Mysterious Disappearances
And Other Strange Tales

Mysterious Disappearances

And Other Strange Tales

By
Ron Quinn

2013
BZB Publishing, Inc.
Tucson, Arizona USA

Mysterious Disappearances
And Other Strange Tales

ISBN-13: 978-1939050045
ISBN-10: 1939050049

Cover and interior photographs and illustrations by Ron Quinn
Little person graphic from "Little People" (Galde Press)
Cover design by Robert Zucker

Published by BZB Publishing, Inc.
P.O. Box 91317
Tucson, Arizona 85752

Printed by CreateSpace, an Amazon.com Company.
Available from Amazon.com, CreateSpace.com and other retail outlets.
Printed in the United States of America.

*Dedicated in Memory of
My brother Charles Quinn,
Walter Fisher and Roy Purdie*

Contents

Introduction

There are many strange stories that just cannot be explained. This is a collection of reported mysterious disappearances, odd happenings, sightings of little people and very strange, unexplained tales.

My mysterious adventure into the unknown began in August 1942. When I was only ten years old, I saw a little man, perhaps a foot tall, standing on a window ledge. It wasn't just an adolescent hallucination.

I continued to be fascinated by unexplained mysteries and other's who had stories of little people. An article about my encounter appeared in an upstate New York weekly paper in 1989. Over the weeks, dozens of letters arrived from people describing their own encounters or similar tales from family members and friends.

The following stories are a glimpse into a world that lies on the fringes of our reality. Only occasionally will these mysteries reveal themselves. This is one of those times…

Ron Quinn

Mysterious Disappearances

A cabin in Upstate New York.

P eople have always been mysteriously disappearing without explanation. Unexplained occurrences and spontaneous disappearances continue to haunt the imagination.

Many have experienced some type of strange encounter with a startling experience– UFO's, ghostly apparitions, aliens and strange paranormal activities.

These are some of the more unusual and odd stories about unexplained disappearances and appearances collected over the decades.

Your Other Half

There are many mysterious tales throughout the world of people who appear for brief moments shortly after sudden death – to bid loved ones goodbye or to warn others of impending danger.

These forms seem to be solid living people and vanish soon afterwards. The following cases illustrate this quite well.

One evening, on a twisting mountain road during 1963, a deadly car accident occurred. Two vehicles hit head on just around a sharp bend. The only casualty was the gentleman driving the sports car.

At that precise moment a man appeared on the road. He was waving his arms and signaling approaching cars that couldn't see the accident around the turn to stop. With this accomplished, he suddenly disappeared.

The individual turned out to be the gentleman who died. Other drivers agreed that the headlights reflected off the man as though he was solid. At his death, this man projected another image of him self to warn others. In doing so, perhaps, he saved others from being killed.

A similar occurrence unfolded south of Tucson, Arizona.

A young man was returning to his mother's home and was hit by a drunken diver. He died instantly at the scene. The time was around nine thirty in the evening.

At that same time, his mother entered her kitchen. Her son was standing near the stove. He smiled and said, "No need to worry, Mom. I'm fine. I love you." He then vanished before her eyes. Several hours later a deputy arrived informing her of the fatality. All who have experienced this claim that the form is solid and not a transparent apparition.

Those who are in a deep sleep or coma also seem to be able to project another image of their self without knowing it.

These following cases are quite interesting.

A Flash of Light

Roy Green has been truck driving for some fifteen years. During this period he witnessed numerous accidents, fires, police chases, etc, along the busy interstates. But this day would be like no other.

While traveling one spring afternoon between Bend and Burns, Oregon on State 20, a white Caddy shot by in the passing lane doing over seventy five. Then slowed, pulling back into the right lane several hundred feet in front of him.

Moments later a bright flash of light filled his cab. It only lasted a second or two before things returned to normal. But, the car had vanished. Roy pulled to the side and stopped. Several cars approaching from the opposite direction did the same.

One driver leaped out shouting, "Damn, did you see that?" Another claimed the flash appeared directly over the Caddy. No sign of the vehicle could be found, not even skid marks. It was like the Caddy never even existed.

Roy, now eighty-one, remembers the incident as though it happened only yesterday. He often wonders, what if the car hadn't pulled in front? Could he have been the one disappearing within the light?

What mysterious force caused this strange phenomenon?

Was it some freak of nature? Or, was it that well known time warp?

Or was some higher intelligence responsible?

Family from the Past

Rick Moore, age sixty-one, moved to Washington state from New Mexico during 1954. After his wife, Sue passed away. He loved the outdoors spending most of his weekends hiking throughout the forests.

During one such trip he followed an old road to its end. It was a picturesque location for camping. Afterward, Rick took a backpack and camera and hiked through the terrain taking pictures and enjoying the mountain scenery. The only sounds were the gentle breeze and occasional bird calls.

A while later, Rick spotted smoke rising above the trees and he headed in that direction. Approaching the area, he saw an old cabin with two young boys stacking firewood. A man was also seen working on a window. Then, a woman emerged from the cabin, stopping beside the door. She wore a long dress with her hair pulled back.

Upon seeing Rick, the lads entered the cabin. Moments later they were seen looking out a window. Walking up, Rick said, "hi," and introduced him self.

Both adults exchanged looks. Then, the man walked up to Rick and said, "Hello there. I'm Dan Hicks, and that's my wife, Mary." She was curious about Rick's clothing and kept looking it over.

Dan asked what he was doing around these parts. Rick replied, "Out hiking and enjoying the surroundings."

Glancing casually about, Rick said jokingly, "You must like this rugged lifestyle to live this primitive. It must be hard on the family." There was no response from Dan.

"How long have you lived here," continued Rick. "Oh, about three years," Dan replied.

Finding it difficult to carry on a lengthy conversation with the gentleman, Rick mentioned he also had two grown boys. Removing a picture from his wallet, Rick passed it to Dan. He looked it over carefully then returned it, saying, "I see you had it colored somehow." It was a strange remark, as if he never had seen a colored photo before.

Looking around once more, Rick said, "Guess I'll return to camp."

"You have a camp nearby?" asked Dan.

Rick answered, "Yes, over by the dirt road just south of here." Dan thought for a moment and replied, "There isn't any road in those parts."

After shaking hands, Rick tipped his hat toward the woman who slightly smiled. Waving at the two boys still peering out the window, he turned and walked off.

Several yards later, he returned again and couldn't believe his eyes. Everything had vanished – the cabin and all. The only things that remained were a few timbers and other debris scattered among the brush.

Rick at first thought that he had imagined the whole thing. But, Rick knew better. He had read many books on UFO's and strange phenomenon, etc. He realized the only answer was that he had somehow stepped through some time warp back into the 1800's. To this day, Rick regrets not taking a picture of the surroundings. He had his camera, but the thought never entered his head.

So moved by the experience, Rick began asking locals about the history of the area. Most told him to visit Old Ed Murphy. He was born and raised in the area.

After telling Ed of his encounter, the old man said, "Others have seen that same family over the years. Back in 1937, several loggers came upon them. Minutes later, everything vanished before their eyes. Most folks around these parts didn't believe their wild yarn until it happened again years later.'

Don and Jean, close friends for over forty years, once visited the alleged location while in eastern Washington during 1957. Several folks in the region heard of Rick but didn't know where he lived. The mysterious area is somewhere near the town of Wenatchee. They spent two days camping there with cameras ready but nothing unusual occurred. Both passed away years ago, and I have no idea what their daughter did with their photo albums as they had pictures of the cabin area.

Some believe that doorways into other times occasionally open by accident for brief periods. One might exist within this location and it might open at random. Rick could have unknowingly entered one when seeing the smoke. Perhaps the family witnessed Rick vanishing as he stepped back into his own time.

I believe there are three sides to time: past, present and future. But all exist at the same moment at different levels.

It sounds incredible, but stories like the above make it believable to those with open minds.

Into Thin Air

During 1900 a small farming community located somewhere in the Midwest was celebrating the Fourth of July. The highpoint of the activities was the annual foot race by the town's younger men.

The run was located on an uneven three-quarter mile, not so perfect, circle. Usually it was. Tall Tom had won due to his long legs.

The runners came around and were heading for the finishing line with Tom, of course, out in front. As they approached the cheering crowd, Tom slipped, falling head first toward the ground.

At that moment, his body became transparent and slowly vanished from view. The crowd gasped in disbelief.

The spot was searched and searched but nothing was ever uncovered that could explain this strange disappearance witnessed by most of the town. A marker was placed where this odd occurrence happened.

Did Tom slip into another dimension or another time? Where could he have gone?

Another mysterious case added to all of the others.

The Elderly Lady

Another remarkable tale occurred during the mid 1950's somewhere in New Jersey. An elderly woman was stumbling about the street and acting confused as if she didn't realize where she was. Her attire resembled that of the 1800's.

A gentleman nearby thought she was sick and ran to assist her. Spotting him approach, the lady yelled, turned and fled up an alley. He followed, calling to her several times but she continued on. Moments later, she vanished before his eyes.

An elderly woman appears acting disorientated, and dressed in period clothing, looks around, yells, and runs off then disappears.

It sounds like our phantom lady was caught in a time warp, and appears in her future. Minutes later while running away, she vanishes back into her own time, or somewhere else? Similar accounts have occurred throughout the world. At any given moment nature's mysterious tricks are perpetrated on her unsuspecting children.

The Giant

About sixty miles northeast of Tepic, Mexico, Ricardo Ortiz had a strange experience back in 1968, so the story goes.

Sometime during mid afternoon while attending his sheep, he noticed the flock acted quite nervous and kept moving around. This had occurred before when a jaguar was in the vicinity.

Later that evening, a great commotion erupted at the corral. Taking his light, Ricardo went to investigate. There was a three quarter moon and visibility was fairly good.

Over where the disturbance occurred a large shadow was seen moving near the trees. It was much too large for a man or bear. In a short time it vanished. Returning to his home, his wife and small son were standing at the door.

Little Felipe pointed toward the tress and said, "Big man. Big man."

Early the next morning, Ricardo discovered one of

his sheep was missing. Also, part of the corral fence was damaged.

Toward evening the sheep once again acted up as darkness approached. Again he stepped outside. To his surprise he spotted the outline of a giant man standing near the edge of the trees. The creature stood some twelve feet high. He was partly clothed and looked as thought he hadn't bathed in years. Long unkempt hair reached below his shoulders. He spotted Ricardo and stepped back among the trees.

Days later he told old Morales, a neighbor, what he had witnessed. The old gentleman said, "Long ago such giants once lived among the mountains. But they had vanished and were never seen again."

Perhaps Little Felipe had seen the large man while playing when he said, "Big man. Big man."

After the first sighting the giant was never seen again. Did he come down from the mountains to visit those of the low lands, then returned to his mountainous retreat? If so, are there others of his species still living in the remote wilderness?

There are tales of giants of this size coming from

the west by boat. They enslaved the local people until one day they acted against them, killing them all. This occurred almost two hundred years ago.

Could a few have escaped? If so, they must have a long life span. There weren't any females among the giants.

Great portions of Mexico are still quite wild. Anything could exist there and go unnoticed for years.

This story was told to us by a Mexican gentleman who living near Nogales, Arizona, back in 1988.

The Hikers

Two experienced outdoorsmen began their day by hiking one of the many trails located in the Santa Catalina Mountains just north of Tucson, Arizona. In the past, both had hiked these narrow picturesque trails and knew these mountains quite well.

Later that day, Bob twisted his ankle badly and couldn't continue. Leaving him beside the trail, his friend, John left for help. At this time, cell phones hadn't been invented.

An hour or so later he returned with Search and Rescue. But there was no sign of Bob. Only his canteen was found near a tree. A lengthy search was made, but no trace of the hiker was ever found.

If there had been a mountain lion attack, which is rare, evidence would have been seen at the site. Besides, he carried side arms.

The question is what had occurred during his friends' absence still remains a mystery.

The Vanishing

This strange disappearance occurred somewhere north of New York. Five friends hiked to a lake for the day. On their return, two were at the rear.

Moving along the trail, George, the last in line, was telling Ted about his daughter. Suddenly he ended his story in mid sentence. Ted turned and George was missing.

A search of the area was made, but no sign of their friend was found. Even after an extended five-day search by authorities, George was never seen again. His disappearance was never solved.

The odd circumstance surrounding this case is that the hiker vanished several feet behind his friend. Ted never heard a sound or witnessed any strange flash of light, nor did the others. Again, could he have stepped into a time warp and might reappear sometime in the future, or the past? Anything is possible in the world of the unknown.

There are also strange forces known as 'dead

space." These open at random and any object entering is instantly disintegrated.

How lucky Ted was. He missed entering this anomaly by several feet.

Vanished in a Second

A bout five years ago a family of four left on a weekend vacation somewhere in the northwest. After locating a suitable campsite the small trailer was parked beside the forest trees.

While his parents and sister, Jill who was ten, fished at the nearby lake. Jimmy, fourteen, explored the surrounding woods.

Later, as the others returned for lunch, they heard the boy shouting, "No, no, I don't want to go," from behind the trailer. Realizing his son was in trouble, the father ran to the scene. Approaching the trailer on the run, Jimmy cried out. "No, no, please."

A split second later the father reached the back of the trailer, but nobody was there. Jimmy and whoever or "whatever" was with him had vanished. Also no sounds came from the surrounding forest.

The father heard his son a moment before arriving

at the scene, yet he had disappeared.

A large search by local authorities uncovered no sign of the boy. It was as though the very earth opened and swallowed him up.

Where could he have gone in that split second, along with what ever was abducting him?

The Union Soldier

This rather unique tale regarding sudden disappearances occurred in Pennsylvania around 1941. This story, however, is quite different then most surrounding these strange events.

Raymond, his wife Mary, and their four-year-old daughter Sue were playing in the city park. Other families were enjoying the surroundings and were scattered throughout the grounds.

Ray rose to retrieve a ball that Sue had thrown and rolled under a nearby park bench. Without a warning, Ray suddenly vanished before their eyes. He was there one second and gone the next. The turmoil it caused most have been unbelievable.

Some ten years later while glancing through a book containing Civil War pictures, Mary spotted her husband standing among Union soldiers.

There was no doubt in her mind. That was her missing Ray.

Examining the photo under a magnifying glass with several friends, it revealed three small moles above the soldiers left eye– the same as her husband. He also had a crooked front tooth as, Ray had, plus other recognizable features. It definitely was Ray.

When he vanished, could he have accidentally stepped into one of these mysterious time warps that open for brief periods then close?

In a park one moment, then perhaps finding himself beside a road or in a farmer's field. It would be impossible to realize what went through his confused mind. Especially when Ray discovered it was 1860 or later. When the shock wore off, he must have accepted his fate.

From the Civil War pictures, it appears he arrived during this conflict. Then, for unknown reasons, he must have joined the Union Army. Did Ray survive this period of history? Or, does he now lie in some unmarked grave along with his companions? If he did survive and married, there has to be a relative somewhere out there.

If this story is true, why didn't Mary come forward with her evidence? Also, no news articles have ever appeared mentioning this remarkable tale.

If the title of the book had been shown, Ray would be known. It would be quite easy to thumb through its pages until finding a soldier with three moles above his left eye and a crooked front tooth.

These strange time portals open and close throughout the world. They remain for brief moments then vanish, carrying their human cargo, if any, to various points of time. They are natural mysterious "one way" time machines, as there are no "return tickets."

A Winter Night

This haunting tale parallels a similar story involving the strange disappearance of a young boy while finishing his nightly chores. Both occurred during a winter evening.

A new layer of snow had fallen covering the grounds around a small rural home. Jerry's job, age twelve, was to empty the ashes from the wood stove and fireplace out behind the woodshed each night.

One evening while carrying the bucket through the snow, his parents heard him yelling. Racing to the back door, his father swung it open but there was no sign of their son. Stepping outside with his wife, both heard him calling from above. His voice became fainter until only silence reached their ears.

On the snow his footprint ended abruptly beside the bucket. It was as though "something" had seized the young lad from above, carrying him off into the dark winter sky.

It couldn't have been any type of bird, as Jerry was large for his size, weighing over seventy-five pounds.

What occurred that night still remains an unsolved mystery? Jerry was never seen again.

The Deadly House

Rick and June were having trouble with their marriage for almost six months. She lived out of town and Rick resided in the city. While visiting one weekend both agreed the relationship was over, as each visit always ended with an argument.

While standing outside her door, June told her husband to leave. Turning, she entered the house closing the door behind her. Before doing so, he entered the house to ask her a question but she wasn't anywhere to be found. The only other door was locked with a chain from the inside. Search as he may, no sign of her could be found.

Rick spent days in his relentless search of the dwelling but never discovered how she had disappeared. June had just vanished into thin air after entering the house.

While feeling depressed over their failed marriage, and her strange disappearance, Rick closed himself in the residence and was never seen again. But this does not end the tale of the mysterious house. Two others also vanished while occupying the home.

During 1858, a teacher accused of being an abolitionist lost her job after thirty years. Feeling alone and unwanted, she also vanished from the odd dwelling.

R. Fisher originally built the house in 1821 for his bride. A year later, she died while giving childbirth. After this occurred he also closed himself within the house and was never seen again.

During the late 1950's I'm told, the house was torn down to make room for a new highway. Over a period of two years several cars traveling this road mysteriously vanished along with their occupants.

Could some unknown force exist in the vicinity where the house once stood? When it activates at random, anything within the area suddenly vanishes. We know many of the small answers regarding the unknown but not the big ones yet.

The Cadet

Three West Point cadets were having a friendly conversation beside the parade grounds. Later, Jeff excused himself and walked away.

Mike suddenly remembered he wanted to ask him something. Turning, he called but there was no sign of him. He couldn't have been more then several yards away when Mike called.

There was no sign of Jeff in any direction. This young future officer was there one second and gone the next. This mysterious disappearance has never been solved.

I doubt that West Point would even acknowledge the incident ever occurred, as some have tried.

Where is Mark?

Anumber of years ago, a strange disappearance happened here in Tucson, Arizona. A father and his three sons were rock hunting out on the desert.

Two of the boys began teasing and fighting with the younger, Mark. After the abuse continued, Mark decided to return to the truck several hundred yards away.

When the others returned there was no sign of Mark. After searching on their own with no success, they called Search and Rescue. Hundreds searched for days, checking every known cave, mineshaft and tunnel.

No trace of the lad was ever found. It was reported that UFO activity was quite heavy in the vicinity of the missing boy several days before his disappearance. I also have known Mark's stepfather since 1963.

The Bungalow

During the spring of 1954, Michael and his family drove to their summer bungalow north of London, England for a pleasant weekend vacation.

The area was a typical English countryside with rolling hills and a nearby stream cutting through their property.

After parking the car near the main entrance, his wife Mary, and daughter Kathy, stepped out and entered the house. Leaving their suitcases beside the open door, Michael parked the auto beside the bungalow.

Gathering the luggage, he entered the residence calling the others. There wasn't any response. He searched, but found no sign of them.

Thinking perhaps they stepped out back, he opened the door and once again called. There was no trace of them. Each had completely vanished. To this day they have never been seen.

Countless others have also mysteriously disappeared from houses, trains and from "planes in flight."

There seems to be no limit to these sudden enigmas of innocent people vanishing instantly while going about there daily activities.

A Micro Second Later

This incredible story appeared only once in the newspapers during 1950. More would have been known of this amazing tale, if it weren't for government intervention.

It all began during 1880 in New York. John Johnson owned a business along what is now Broadway in New York City. After closing his establishment for the night, he walked several blocks to his home, but never arrived. The gentleman was never heard of again. A short article appeared in the local paper about his strange disappearance.

Now let's step forward seventy years to Broadway 1950. Theater lights blinked throughout the area, people covered the sidewalks and cars sounded their horns. It was a typical Saturday evening along Broadway and Forty Second Street.

Suddenly, a man appeared in the middle of traffic. He acted confused and terrified. A moment later, a truck hit him and knocked the gentleman into the patch of another vehicle and killed him.

At the Coroner's Office, things turned into puzzlement. The victim was dressed in 1880 attire. He also carried money from that period. In his pocket they discovered receipts with his name and dated, November 1880. It was as if he just arrived from the distant past.

Also present was a news reporter who wrote an article about the strange gentleman and his appearance.

Suggesting, jokingly, it looked as though he arrived from the past.

A woman at the local library, a Reference Librarian, remembered reading an old article about a John Johnson disappearing after seeing the story written by the reporter. A lengthy investigation revealed that both Johnson's were the same.

Later, the government became interested and confiscated the body, along with all items he carried. By now, the story was out. But, government agents still told all involved to "forget the incident ever occurred."

Mr. Johnson walks home after closing his business. He crosses the street and then finds himself in 1950. Can you imagine the terror he must have experienced? Suddenly standing among moving objects perhaps hundreds of people moving about and thousands of flashing lights. Surely he must have thought he was in hell itself.

It seems he accidentally entered a time portal and stepped seventy years into the future. The gentleman, while crossing the street, was somehow catapulted into one century within the blink of an eye. Also, why was our government so interested in this story?

The Healer

During our adventurous trip to Arizona 1956-57 we moved camp to Prescott, a small peaceful community, for the summer months.

Every three weeks, Chuck, Roy, Walt and I drove to town for supplies. After these chores were accomplished, we relaxed in the city park beneath the shady trees before we returned to camp some ten miles away.

During these little breaks we occasionally met locals from the area. One was Ray Morehead. He had moved to Prescott shortly after the war. He enjoyed hearing our tales of adventures. Especially the stories of lost mines and buried treasures allegedly hidden throughout the southwest.

Smiling, Ray said, "I have a beauty of a story, but it hasn't anything to do with treasures. I know you'll find it mind boggling, as I and others witnessed the entire miracle.

One summer back in Lewisburg, Pennsylvania, I was shopping on a Friday night. The streets were crowded and traffic was heavy. While waiting to cross the street, a woman and her daughter stepped off the curb without looking. A car hit both throwing them into the air like rag dolls. The girl took the blunt of the impact. It killed her instantly.

I ran over as others followed. The mother wasn't hurt too much. But, the girl had a deep gash across her forehead and a broken leg.

The poor mother was holding her, screaming, "She's dead. My little girl is dead." Talk about bringing tears to your eyes. It was a dreadful scene to see.

There were some ten or more people standing around. Several women tried to comfort her but to no avail.

From out of the crowd a man appeared, perhaps in his mid thirties. He wore light tan boots, trousers and a turtleneck sweater of the same color. He knelt beside the woman, saying, "Your daughter is not dead, only sleeping." He then places one hand on her leg injury and the other on her face. Within seconds a white light appeared beneath his palms.

When removed the injuries had vanished. The only sound heard was a sudden gasp of disbelief from the crowd.

Several voices were heard saying, "It's a miracle!" "My God, what did he do?" A number of women fell to their knees crossing themselves.

The gentleman rose and walking off, some called out, "Hey, who are you?"

"Don't leave," said another, "The authorities would want to talk to you." (I bet they would.)

Several tried following him but were lost among the onlookers. When the police and ambulance arrived, the scene was in turmoil. Everyone was talking at once. Police were asking questions and firemen were examining the little girl. The mother stood holding her daughter, but there wasn't an injury on her. Even the blood covering her face and dress had vanished.

The girl looked somewhat bewildered at all the activity going on around her. Moments later both left in the ambulance.

A day later, the story was on the radio. At first, it was treated as serious news. Some thought it was a hoax or joke. What became of the girl wasn't known. Each hospital denied having her as a patient."

There were several theories. One was that the stranger was her guardian angel. There are thousands of fatal accidents each year. These people were not visited by their guardian angle and saved. Why was this girl chosen? Perhaps it wasn't her time to die and a mistake was made. But remember, God does not make mistakes.

The Vanishing Plane

S ome tales are difficult to believe. Perhaps this story falls into that category. On the other hand, it might possibly be true. Other similar cases have been reported around the world.

I believe this occurred sometime back in the late 1949, or so. A passenger plane was carrying military personnel home for the holidays. It disappeared between Seattle and Alaska. Its wreckage has never been found.

A story that was making the rounds in Lower Canada was about a miner or trapper who had a strange experience, but few believed his tale. His name escapes me, so lets call him Hank.

During the time of the disappearance, Hank was living near the route most planes travel. One afternoon while feeding livestock, he spots a large plane approaching from the north. All at once a loud band was heard. Looking skyward he saw smoke coming from the craft. His first thought was, "Oh, those poor people."

The plane turned over heading nose first toward the ground. About 1,500 feet before impact the craft slowly vanished. Seconds later, the sky was clear. It was completely gone.

Others in the community didn't believe his wild tale. Most thought old Hank was dreaming or drunk. But remember, this plane did disappear without a trace.

A Strange Encounter

While at the library researching a story of the Peck Ranch massacre by Apaches during 1886, I happened to meet, John Owen, age in the late sixties or so.

I often keep several copies of my book, *Little People* (Galde Press) on hand. In doing so, I've managed to sell a few. John spotted my name on the cover, asking if I was the author, and I nodded yes. After thumbing through the pages, John asked if I'd be interested in hearing about a weird experience he had back in 1991.

Always on the look out for new material, whether it's about tales of the strange or about Arizona's wild past, I answered, yes.

For three years, John lived on the streets of Hollywood, California. Before straightening his life out several years later. He knew some "street smart" individuals who taught him the ways of survival.

All three shared an alley off Hollywood

Boulevard. John would have a drink with his friends, but never became intoxicated where his reasoning was impaired. His last drink was mid afternoon and it was past eight at night. The others were off somewhere and were expected back shortly.

According to John, every word of this wild tale is true. John sat beside several large trashcans. A little light came from above near the corner of a building.

While relaxing on his bedroll thinking where the remainder of his life was going, he noticed a short fat man perhaps three and a half feet tall walking up the alley coughing his head off. He passed John's location not noticing him among the shadows.

Placing both hands against the wall, the odd little man began coughing louder and more violently. In the dim light, John saw the gentleman's features. He had shiny eyes, no hair and a round face. Also, the corners of his mouth almost reached his ears. Giving him an extreme wide mouth.

All at once another little guy, some eighteen inches tall "POPS" out of his mouth landing on the pavement below. This fellow also starts coughing, and a smaller guy "POPS" out of his mouth.

This one is about seven inches high. All three began talking and examining some round object they pass among themselves. The little one had a high squeaky, thrilling voice, and kept running in circles.

Gazing in disbelief at the weird scene unfolding before him, John decided to stand up. Upon seeing him all began returning back into each other. The smallest one jumps back into the other's mouth. He in turn leaps back into the fat one's wide mouth.

He then turns, running up the alley. Not seeing a way out he turns facing John, with a look of horror on his face. He then sprouts bird like wings, flying off over the buildings, John said. All wore clothing of the Renaissance period.

At that moment the others returned and John relates the wild tale to them. However, one did "see" something large flying up from the darkened alley.

John kept insisting he wasn't dreaming, drunk or

on drugs. What he experienced actually occurred to him. Try as I may, I couldn't convince him what he witnessed couldn't exist.

After pulling himself out of the streets four years later, John found a good job and returned to a normal life style. But, that strange night in the alley remains with him always. Like it happened only yesterday. Just as the folks who have seen the little people of the Catskill Mountains of New York. That experience also remains with you forever.

Do other worlds and dimensions exist nearby and occasionally slip over into ours by accident for brief moments as in the two stories of my book, *Little People*; "The Phantom Forest" and "Incident at Neversink." If my memory is correct, I believe I read something similar to John's tale. It might have been in a book on Greek Mythology. Something about a giant coughing up ugly little monsters.

Is the story told by, John true? I hope so, as it would make life more interesting. Never knowing what we'll encounter as we travel down the bumpy road of life.

The Mystery Street

During September 1980, Larry Green, a merchant marine, drove to see his sister that evening. He would be leaving the following day for California. She lived in Flushing, New York. Larry was back east visiting her and several friends.

Stopping for a traffic light, Larry noticed all the cars were late 1930s and early '40s models. Thinking a vintage car show was in town, he thought no more about it.

Several cars pulled beside him and both the drivers and passengers kept looking his car over with great curiosity. At the time, Larry was driving a '78 Ford.

Approaching another light, he stopped again. People on the curb started gathering around his car with puzzled expressions. Several looked at Larry quite strangely than walked off. All wore clothing from the '40s or earlier, according to Larry.

Moving on, he began noticing little changes from

days before - the lighting, signs and especially the billboards along the route. One had advertisements that hadn't been seen in years.

Reaching the street his sister lived on he turned left and parked in front of her home. After relating this amazing story, both couldn't arrive at a satisfactory answer.

The following morning, Larry kissed her goodbye and left for the west coast. The street from the night before again looked normal. No old cars, people wearing out of date attire or billboards advertising products from the past.

Larry told his remarkable story to our friend, Roy, also a merchant marine while at the Seamens Union in San Francisco around 1993.

Did Larry and his car somehow slip back to the 1940's for a brief moment in time? No wonder people were astonished at seeing his '78 Ford rolling down their street.

Is this story true? Roy thinks so, as he had shipped out with Larry many times. Roy believed he was an honest truthful person. How Larry arrived there and returned is one of natures' little secrets.

Now A Believer

A Forest Ranger, a disbeliever in the existence of Big Foot, once had an encounter he'll never forget. It occurred somewhere along the Columbia River in Washington State.

While patrolling along the banks of this river, he heard some sounds near trees by the waters edge. Expecting to find children fishing, he climbed down the embankment to investigate.

Stepping around the corner of the trees, he came face to face with a Bigfoot. He froze in his tracks as both eyed each other. The creature stood nearly eight feet high, and was less then ten feet away.

After several seconds, it turned and lumbered off down stream. Later, he said, the thing must have weighed close to four hundred pounds.

It might have been his imagination. But he said, "I heard the ground rumble as it moved away."

Today the Ranger is a true believer in the legend of

these mysterious creatures that have been seen for nearly two hundred years - even earlier than that - if one believes the stories told by local Indians.

Many claim if Big Foot does exist, why haven't any skeletal remains been discovered? Bears outnumber them, and their remains, I believe, have never been found.

I've Come to Take You Home

Kingston, New York is located along the banks of the Hudson River. During the mid 40's, a strange thing occurred near this town. Then, and perhaps even today, a home for girls was run by Episcopal Nuns. Most of the girls were from broken homes or had other problems.

Bobby's mother was hospitalized for several weeks and his Dad worked. They were looking for some place where their son could stay. The mother knew a Nun at St. John's Hospital. She spoke to the Mother Superior at the home. She agreed to take the boy for that length of time, even though it was a place for girls.

Bobby was surrounded by giggling obnoxious females who resented he was there. A few Sisters felt the same.

Out back was a large play area that had a hill some ten feet high. It was mid winter and snow covered the ground. Bobby's job was to haul the slides back up the hill so the little devil girls, as he called them, could slide down. When anything bad happened, they pointed to Bobby saying, "It was his fault."

Naptime was a nightmare. During the afternoon, he was rolled up in a blanket like a hotdog and placed on the bed. This was to prevent him from getting up. Only his head and feet were seen.

This indignity lasted for an hour each afternoon. Bobby knew he'd be in deep trouble if nature called. How he wished his Dad would come taking him away from this daily routine of nasty girls, slave labor and occasional insults.

By the middle of the second week (Wednesday), Bobby thought of running away. Late that afternoon, he was alone in his room feeling quite despondent. Suddenly, the door opened and his father came in.

Smiling, he said. "Hi son, I've come to take you home." Bobby ran into his arms. Looking up, his Dad had vanished. He wasn't anywhere to be found. When telling the Sisters what happened, he was accused of lying. That meant washing dishes for two days. Poor Bobby just couldn't win.

When Sunday arrived, his Dad came to his room. Smiling, he said. "Hi son, I've come to take you home."

While on the train, Bobby told his Dad about seeing him Wednesday afternoon. His father looked somewhat shocked upon hearing this. On that same day while going home from work, he fell asleep on the train and dreamed he was visiting Bobby in his room. To him it was quite real.

Did he somehow project a second image of himself into the room and took on a three-dimensional form his son could touch?

I have read of similar cases over the years. It demonstrates how wonderful and marvels the human mind is. Perhaps someday in the dim future we might understand it's full potential.

The Mysterious Craft

O ld "Tata Joe," meaning 'Grandfather' in Spanish, lived on the Papago Indian Reservation west of Tucson, Arizona.

Over the years he told us many stories, legends and interesting facts about his ancient people. Joe had those classic features of an old Indian.

Being a cowboy most of his adult life, his face resembled leather left out on the dry desert from riding the range under the Arizona sun.

This incident occurred sometime during 1960 while returning home on State Highway 86 and crossing the desert flats, also known as Altar Valley. Joe noticed something odd off toward the north. It resembled three large silver spheres, one atop the other. The object was perhaps half a mile away.

Joe took a dirt road leading in that general direction. The thing was now on his left as he approached. Stopping several hundred feet from the strange machine he walked the remaining distance.

Nobody was around and the thing had no openings. As he came closer, Joe heard a light humming sound coming from within. He circled the towering monolith before him that was almost thirty feet in height. Each sphere was about ten feet across and attached to each other. It sat on four short pyramid shaped legs.

At first he thought it might be some machine for drilling wells but no other equipment was seen. Old Joe, having a curious nature most of his adult life, approached and touched its surface. It felt more like plastic then steel. As he did so, the humming increased. The object rose slowly making no sound. In seconds it disappeared among the clouds.

Was anybody inside the craft seen by Joe? Or was it operated by remote control? When Joe touched the surface it might have sent a signal alerting some intruder was nearby. If so, it could have been someone's "Space Probe" from "out there," or ours. Joe also mentioned that the ground beneath where the object stood was warm to the touch.

While telling others of his weird experience, several said they also had seen the mysterious machine while in the desert the last few weeks.

In the foothills of the Tumacacori Mountains, some forty odd miles south of this location, a hiker claimed to have seen the same type of craft as described by Joe. It stood among some trees near Bear Grass Lake, a watering hole for local cattle.

There are a number of hot spots throughout Arizona where UFO's seem to congregate. Why would one land out on the desert where there is only hot winds, heat, sand, desolation and bad tempered varmints crawling about?

Half Human

Back in 1940, two brothers, Mark and Ken along with a friend, were fishing in the waters off Nova Scotia. Their rig was a twenty-foot boat. The catch for the day was great, so they decided to head back to shore.

Off port side they caught sight of something large in the water. It would suddenly appear then submerge, only to surface on the starboard side. Whatever it was remained just below the surface. With the rolling of the boat it was difficult to determine it's size.

While gathering up their gear, the thing appeared nearby looking directly at them. They were shocked by its appearance. The face looked almost human. It had a nose and small mouth, and gills were noticed on both sides. It once again dove beneath the water then rose several feet above the surf.

It was yellow-green in color and scales covered most of its body. Ken swore the creature had arms and hands. All at once two others surfaced beside the first one. They looked toward the crew and disappeared under the sea. It was estimated their bodies were perhaps the size of a small teenager.

They realized that they would be ridiculed to reveal what they saw. It was decided not to mention the sighting with anyone, including their families.

A week later while at the same location, the three sea creatures appeared again. Not showing any hostility toward the men, they swam closer. They noticed how intelligent these strange things looked. Ken was correct. They had arm like limbs with fingers.

For several more weeks the sea visitors would come and go. One time, the largest of the three approached the boat and threw a seashell lightly on-board. Was this a sign of friendship, or did it have another meaning? One day, the creatures just vanished and were never seen again.

Sometime later, another fisherman told a tale of seeing something strange in the waters off the coast. It looked half human, was yellow in color and had arms. Only then Mark and the others told of their encounter with the creatures.

Were these mutants created accidentally by nature, or were they aliens living beneath the sea looking us over?

This story reminds me of that motion picture, "The Abyss." Roy, a merchant marine, told us this strange tale many years before the picture was released. He heard this story while shipping out to the orient during the late sixties.

These men of the sea tell many stories. Could this one be true?

If so, where did these marvelous creatures come from? We know so little about that strange world beneath the sea.

The Desert Mirage

During summer of 1964, Dave and Peggy W. were returning from visiting friends in New Mexico. Their route was through southern Arizona.

Near the town of Willcox there is a large desolate dry lake many miles wide. Scarce of trees and vegetation, it's a barren place of nothingness where several western movies have been filmed.

As they drove parallel to this lonely stretch of desert, Dave glanced toward his left. About two miles away above the floor of the dry lake appeared a mountain range where none should be.

Scattered below on the rolling hills were odd shaped houses and other buildings. Also a lake was nearby. Beside the water rose a high rocky escarpment. At its summit stood a castle. It resembled those seen in Europe but was, more modern in appearance. A flag flew from a tower but was too far off to make out its design. No people could be noticed among the dwellings.

Dave drew his wife's attention to the odd scene.

He then pulled to the side of the road and stopped.
Moments later another car stopped. This individual
began taking pictures of the strange mirage.

The entire scene had a fairy world appearance.
Even the towering mountains projected serenity.
Other mirages have appeared over this location.
But where did this mysterious one originate? From
across the sea, or from a land still undiscovered?

Both agreed they had never seen such architectural
design. The outer walls slanted inward. The first
level was perhaps ten feet high. On the roof was a
round section, and above were one or more domes.
All were white, including the castle. This beautiful
picturesque scene lasted perhaps five minutes
before it slowly faded from view.

Some mirages at this location have shown coastal
water scenes of other countries and Mexico.
Wherever this peaceful valley exists surely wasn't
on this earth. Perhaps we weren't meant to view
this place and it was another mistake of nature.

Just like the mysterious plateau I wrote of near the
Mexican border it juggles time around at random
and still remains an unsolved mystery.

On our last visit to this oddity of nature, some jumping, crackling sparks were noticed nearby our campsite. The following morning a photo of that area was taken. It's covered with crystals, quartz, broken geodes and stones. It's a strange location. What you might see one time will be gone the next time your there. This freak of nature plays with time as a child with a ball. It bounces from place to place.

One must be careful while visiting this upside down plateau. Anything might occur at any moment. Out of all of my visits, I've only witnessed one strange occurrence.

Returning to the mirage. The pictures taken by the other party never appeared, I was told, in any magazine or newspaper. Perhaps his camera lens didn't capture the remarkable scene. If not, why?

The Indian Stones

One time, our friend Louie Romero told us of some Indian signs he found. They were carved on nine black stones the size of bowling balls and formed a semi circle. These were located at the junction of Murphy and Apache Canyon on the hill northeast of the junction. The stones had stick figures cut into them along with various animals and petroglyphs.

They were first found in 1949 and last seen three years later while rounding up cattle. One afternoon we drove down Apache and arrived at the site shortly after. We climbed the hillside as we searched, but we didn't find any stones as described by Louie. Perhaps he was mistaken. So the other hills were checked. Still, no Indian stones were found. There were no rock formations nearby consisting of black stone in the vicinity, only broken lava. It's possible they were carried from another location and placed at this site for religious ceremonies.

Some hunters or hikers might have stumbled upon them and hauled them off. It's a shame those who found these bits of history (including Chuck) have removed them for personal use. Perhaps they are decorating someone's flower garden. This occurs quite frequently. This is the reason I haven't revealed the locations of several mysterious sites, including the great Indian wall.

Chuck learned his lesson concerning the Indian pots. I wonder if those responsible for removing the stones hear distant drums and rattle sticks at night.

The Coin and
the Chicken

This incredible story into the world of the unknown was told to me back in the mid 1970's. This unexplainable event happened to his neighbor's wife one Saturday afternoon.

We'll call her Pat, as her real name escapes me after all of these years.

Pat was in the kitchen cleaning a fresh chicken on the drain board beside the sink. Just below in the corner stood the kitchen wastebasket. Everything was normal. No strange lights, odd sounds, or feelings of impending danger, was felt. It was a typical afternoon in the house.

While cutting the chicken, it slipped from her grasp falling into the corner. Looking, she couldn't locate it. Thinking it might have fallen into the basket, Pat searched. Still, there was no chicken. She looked everywhere it could have slid. But again, it wasn't found.

After informing her husband, he joined the search.

This phantom chicken had completely vanished. After telling several close friends of this weird experience. Most couldn't provide a logical answer to the mystery.

Pat often felt uneasy while in the kitchen alone. She didn't want to approach the corner where this unusual event happened. She placed a tall stool there that nobody ever used.

About three weeks later while at the sink, Pat heard something hit then bounce off the wooden stool. Looking down she spotted a coin near her feet. She picked it up. The coin felt rather "warm." It turned out to be a Spanish coin made of silver and dated somewhere around the mid 1700's.

Several weeks later, the house was put up for sale. The new owners only laughed upon hearing the tale of the disappearing chicken and falling coin. It is not known whether any strange activities occurred to the new owners.

Pat and her husband moved to the northwest section of Tucson. After being in their new home several weeks, small rocks began hitting their house. Police were called a number of times. But, nobody ever was found throwing them. This began to occur quite frequently.

No pranksters were found. Several people searched the desert area while the rocks rained down on the roof. The falling rocks stopped after a couple of weeks.

Did someone or "something" want their coin back and followed them to their new residence? Did the chicken fall accidentally into a parallel world, or different time? Also, why a Spanish coin? We know so little about the unknown that surrounds us.

Miracle on the Mountain

A young rock climber by the name of Michael from California had an incredible experience while on a sheer mountainside. Since he resembled actor, Sylvester Stallone, some friends nicknamed him, Rocky, the Rock Climber.

He was well experienced with his hobby and scaled many high cliffs throughout the West. It was a dangerous, but a thrilling sport. One mistake and it was all over. This is his remarkable story.

While on vacation one summer in Montana, Michael decided to climb one such rocky escarpment where others occasionally climb. The towering face of stone leaned inward approximately ten degrees from vertical. The height was some hundred and eighty feet.

On the craggy face of the cliff about a hundred feet up was a natural small cave. It was large enough for a single climber and was used by some to rest before they continued upward.

They arrived at the site at ten in the morning, Michael prepared for the climb. Some twenty minutes later he arrived parallel with the cave and found himself in deep trouble.

Being only five foot eight, he couldn't quite reach the next handhold just above his head. Both feet were secure in their footing. He stretched to reach the small nodule that protruded from the wall. He slipped and fell away from the granite face. He realized that death was but seconds away. Michael closed his eyes and prayed. But, something was wrong.

He found himself floating in mid air several feet from the rock wall. He looked downward. There was nothing beneath his feet but empty space.

Michael felt himself move toward the cave some ten feet away. After he reached it, he grabbed one edge, and pulled himself to safety.

Not believing what had just occurred, he sat there breathing quite heavily. What happened, he thought, was surely an act of God. After he rested for several minutes, Michael knew he had to finish the climb.

He arrived at the summit and followed the path on the other side back down to the staging area and his truck. He collapsed and began to shake. The realization of what occurred on the mountain finally began to sink in.

To this day, Michael believes his escape from death was attributed to the crucifix he wore around his neck. It once belonged to his Great, Great Grandmother who lived in Italy.

As he floated mysteriously, the cross and chain was straight out in front of him, as if somebody was holding it to prevent him from falling.

As he pulled him self into the narrow cave, the cross and chain both dropped to his chest.

Michael no longer rock climbs since he reached fifty. He also never removes the cross from around his neck, which he believes saved his life on that frightful day.

Those two famous words, "IF ONLY" come into play here. If only another party was with him, say, filming his climb from below when he fell and floated in mid air. What a wonderful sight that would have been, if it was caught on film.

Three Strange Tales of the Sea

R oy Purdie, friend and partner for over forty years, was also a merchant marine. When not exploring with us he could be found aboard a ship visiting interesting ports.

During these years on the sea, he heard many mysterious tales about the haunted waters of the South Pacific from other shipmates.

One time while on the orient run, Roy had the opportunity to encounter his first experience with the unknown. The crewmember on watch that night spotted a large circular light on the waters off the portside. The bright light was perhaps three hundred yards away.

Others, including Roy, moved to the deck railing for a better view. The object was some thirty feet in diameter and several feet beneath the surface. Slowly it moved aft of the ship about a hundred and fifty yards closer. Suddenly three small spheres appeared out of the water. They paused momentarily in the sky. Then they shot off toward the north and vanished from view.

Two members of the crew had taken pictures. But the films' ASA rating was far too low to capture any sharp image. All that appeared on the finished prints was a faint light.

If Roy said it happened, it did. He and his friend, Walt, was one of the finest people you could meet. When God made those two, he broke the mold afterwards.

Story 2

While on the Alaskan run during the summer of '64, Johnny the Wanderer, as some shipmates called him told the following story to Roy.

One evening just after sundown, Johnny was on deck. A light fog encircled the ship, but visibility was still quite good.

From out of the mist a dark three mast sailing ship appeared. It looked old and ragged. Its sails were full but there was no breeze. It moved across the water leaving no wake behind.

Four others also saw the phantom ship slip silently by. Moments later it vanished among the fog. Was it a ghost ship or their imagination? No way, said Johnny. All shipmates described the same scene.

Story 3

During the closure of World War II, Roy was off the coast of Australia. One afternoon, Roy and others saw a large silver gray ball some fifty feet in diameter rise from the ocean. It hung suspended above the water then moved off rapidly toward the west.

Do we have a colony of aliens living beneath our oceans? If so, are they here visiting and studying our ways? I would like to see their report on us.

In a world of pollution, greed, mistrust and making war with our neighbors constantly, on a scale of one through ten, we surely would be a "one."

The Mysterious Rock House

T he Tascosa Mountains parallel the Mexican border of Southern Arizona. This rugged unfriendly region is cut with numerous canyons, craggy cliffs and legends.

One particular story was told by A.J. Allen, a long time resident of Arivaca, a desert village located in the shadows of the mysterious Tumacacori Range.

A. J., as most called him, was an old time prospector and miner. He was also quite reliable and honest.

While out among the Tascosa's, around 1950, he came upon a canyon he hadn't explored before. Hiking up its rocky bed, A.J. soon came to a pass leading upward. Reaching the halfway point he arrived at a ledge that couldn't be seen from below. It measured some thirty by twenty feet. An old rock cabin was built beside the cliff face.

The door was partly open, so he entered. It was furnished with table, a chair, clothing, canned goods and various other items. Above the crude fireplace hung a rifle. Outside a small corral was beside the cabin and fresh horse droppings were lying around.

A.J. knew most of the prospectors living in the out-of-the-way places. But, he never met anyone from this lonely part of the world. He left, thinking he might meet the owner during his return trip back down the canyon, but he didn't. Whoever lived there might be working a mining claim somewhere in the area.

Several weeks later while talking with another miner, Charley Bent, he mentioned finding the rock cabin. Old Bent was curious to see the site, so a return trip was made.

The canyon was found and, later, the pass. But something was different. It was overgrown and looked as though it hadn't been used for a considerable length of time.

Reaching the ledge, A.J. couldn't believe his eyes. The cabin was there, but the roof had caved in, and one wall had collapsed. Also, a mesquite tree was growing through a window. The ruins appeared to be quite old. The items within the cabin were rotted and scattered around. The rifle above the fireplace was still there. My brother Chuck and I saw it while visiting A. J. during our two year Treasure hunting odyssey. [1]

When A.J. came upon the ledge did he somehow step through a time warp back into the past like others have throughout the centuries?

Around 1937, a gentleman living in Tubac, Arizona, another small community near the Tucson-Nogales Highway heard the above story.

It brought back memories of a tale he heard from a relative. A friend of the family came to Arizona to seek his fortune. One letter mentioned he had discovered a rich silver mine. Later, he built a rock house on a ledge high above the valley. The mine was located south of Peck Canyon. This occurred in 1918. What became of the gentleman isn't known.

Here we have A.J. discovering a new rock house with "fresh horse droppings." Three weeks later, it's showing age and in ruins. There is but one answer. Those mysterious doorways into other

---

[1] "Searching for Arizona's Buried Treasures," by Ron Quinn, 2013. Available from Amazon.com.

time periods open at random.

Perhaps, the miner had an accident while he worked his claim and died never to see his cabin again. If the ledge has been found by anyone else over the years, surely the rifle would have been taken.

A.J. and Charley often said. "It's one hell of a mystery we'll never understand."

The Package

Irene G. enjoyed shopping by catalog and did so for many years. While she glanced through a new one she checked off four items that interested her.

She planned to send for them later in the week. But, two days later, a delivery service knocked at her door and handed Irene a package. After she signed for it, she placed the box on a table.

Irene couldn't imagine who sent it. She wasn't expecting any shipments. When it was opened, she discovered the four items she intended to order.

She checked the company name on the catalog and the label. They were the same. Irene called the company and asked who had ordered the items for her. There was no record of such an order. Had she mistakenly placed the order and forgot? No transactions were on her credit card. They also had no record of the purchase.

She removed the shipping label and made a copy to send the original to the company. Their reply: there was no record of the shipment on file.

Now, comes the shocker. A week later, after she received the package, the box, label and all four items vanished from her home. After this occurred, Irene reordered the items and received them several weeks later.

You're a better person than I am if you can figure this mystery out. That also goes for all her friends and neighbors.

Stepping Through Time

There is another fascinating story of "accidental time travel" few have heard, I've been told. Whether it's true will be up to the reader. I myself have mixed opinions.

I heard this interesting tale some fifteen years ago and only remember the high points.

Back in 1850, a gentleman owned a flourishing livery stable on the corner of New York City, what is now Broadway. After he locked up for the night, he made his way home several blocks away. This gentleman, we'll name Harry Townsend, never arrived at his residence.

A lengthy search was made but the man was never seen again. It has been suspected that he met with foul play. Perhaps he was robbed, killed and buried. He was listed as missing in police files.

Let us now leap forward a hundred years to 1950. Broadway was now a busy street of theaters, restaurants, thousands of lights, honking cars and confusion. The time was approximately seven thirty in the evening.

All at once a man appeared in the middle of traffic. He looked frightened, disoriented and confused running among the cars.

Suddenly, a truck hit him and instantly killed the man. His body was taken to the local Coroner's Office. He was examined, but a strange sight greeted them.

The man wore new clothing of the 1800's. He had gold and silver coins on his person and a letter from his sister. It was postmarked August 1850.

Everyone was quite puzzled. It was as if the gentleman had just arrived from the past.

A young investigative reporter with an inquisitive nature was also there. He realized that he had the makings of a strange story. He came up with a wild idea.

He knew many in local government and somehow obtained old records of that period. After several days of searching he found the same name, Harry Townsend, as it appeared on the old envelope. This was listed under missing persons of 1850.

He was about to write his amazing theory of the possibility that this gentleman somehow stepped through time into 1950.

Across town another unusual occurrence was unfolding. Several government men arrived at the Coroner's Office and demanded the release of the body. Also, our reporter was told not to write his story, or mention his theory to anybody.

Rumor has it the mysterious story once appeared in some newspaper or magazine many years later.

It appears our gentleman was crossing his quiet street and somehow passed through a time warp sending him into the future of 1950.

Can you imagine how he felt – suddenly appearing among cars, noise, flashing lights and hundreds of people. Surely, he must have thought he was in hell itself.

Why did the government want his body? Perhaps they wanted to erase all signs of the accident and didn't want the story published about a man who traveled through time to present day New York.

Keep the truth from the public. Lie, intimidate and hush things up. But, never tell the truth.

"Governments might change, but the lies remain the same," a quote from a "James Bond" film.

Where Are They?

Where Are They? [2]

This strange disappearance occurred somewhere in New York state. I cannot recall all the details surrounding this case, but perhaps it's still remembered in the vicinity of where it happened.

A group of five or six campers had taken off early one morning from their campsite for a hike through the forest. They followed a trail that wound lazily through the timber. Around noon, they stopped for lunch and rested beneath some shady trees. During this break, some took pictures while others engaged in small talk.

Afterwards, the small party headed back to camp about six miles distant. Several walked together while others hiked alone. They were stretched out perhaps thirty feet as they moved down the picturesque trail. Little did they realize the day would come to a mysterious and frightful end.

The individual next to the last member was about

2 *"Where Are They?"* is reprinted from Ron Quinn's "Little People."

ten feet ahead of his companion. During their journey the two talked occasionally about various subjects. The hiker turned to answer a question George had just asked, but he was nowhere to be seen.

After calling him and receiving no reply, the hikers spread out and searched the immediate area, but couldn't locate the missing man. There were no hidden holes along the route, nor any deep ravines he could have fallen into.

After his disappearance was reported, a large search party descended on the area and began their intense search. They never found the missing hiker.

To this day the gentleman has never been located. The odd circumstance surrounding this case is that the hiker vanished within several feet of his friend. Where he disappeared to I guess will never be answered. Perhaps, he stepped through some kind of time warp, and will reappear sometime in the future. Or perhaps, he vanished into the past.

There is some speculation about small doorways that open and close at random. By some, these are known as "dead spaces." Anything caught within them would be disintegrated instantly. These areas could also be doorways into other dimensions. It sounds a little like science fiction, but something is making people vanish suddenly.

This brings to mind another vanishing that occurred during the 1960s. A family of four left on a two-day fishing trip.

After locating a suitable campsite near the river, they parked their small trailer beside some trees. Later, the parents and daughter went fishing. Jimmy, their fourteen-year-old son, wasn't feeling well and decided to remain at the trailer. As the family was returning for lunch they heard Jimmy shouting from behind the trailer.

"No! No, leave me alone! I don't want to go!" They thought somebody might be trying to kidnap the boy. The father dropped his fishing rod ran to his son's aid. As he reached the rear, he again heard the boy cry out, "No, no, please!" A split second later the father rounded the corner, and was surprised to find nobody there.

He had heard the boy a moment before, yet he had vanished instantaneously. They searched but never found him. Authorities were called and they came up empty-handed. The young lad had vanished off the face of the earth. Jimmy was there one second and gone the next.

There are numerous disappearances like this that have occurred throughout the world. Strange and unexplainable things do happen almost every year, and few, if any, appear in national newspapers. If they do appear in print, it's usually in local papers where the incident occurred.

We had something like the above happen in Tucson, Arizona many years ago. The boy was seen returning to his dad's truck on the desert. He was visible one second and gone the next. Hundreds searched for days but he also was never seen again. I knew his stepfather personally.

Strange New York

Strange New York [3]

Another odd occurrence worth mentioning happened to a young boy of fourteen during a cold winter many years ago. This also took place in northern New York, so the story goes.

This tale might be found sandwiched between reality and that famous "zone" most of us have seen on television.

The boy and his older brother would take turns emptying the ashes from the kitchen stove and fireplace. These were placed near the pump hose, about fifty feet from the rear door. Most of the time this task was finished by late afternoon or by early evening.

One night, Billy didn't get around to the chore until quite late. It was cold and silent outside. Large, fluffy white clouds dotted the dark winter sky. Billy picked up the buckets of ash and

---

3 "Strange New York" is reprinted from Ron Quinn's book, *"Little People."*

shuffled his way toward the dumpsite. The only sound to reach his ears was the crunching of the frozen snow beneath his feet. As he reached the halfway point, Bill happened to look skyward and froze in fear. Floating above the trees about sixty yards away was the giant head of an old, bearded man.

Billy's description of the weird apparition was quite vivid.

It resembled some kind of Greek god. The face had two dark holes for eyes and a large, sneering mouth that opened and closed as the menacing head rocked back and forth. It looked as if it was laughing, but no sound came forth from the ghostly figure. The face had strong features and its beard and hair consisted of long, flowing curls.

Bill dropped both buckets and ran screaming toward the house. He slipped and fell several times on the way. His parents and brother heard the ruckus and reached the door just as he came flying through, yelling about a giant head in the night sky.

When he finally persuaded them to look outside, all that was visible were a few clouds, but none resembled any hideous head. His father said he must have mistaken a cloud for the head, and his eyes played tricks on him.

Billy insisted it wasn't a cloud. Besides, the head was not over the pump house where a few clouds remained, but near the trees toward the right, where no clouds could be seen.

Other Strange Tales

Photo of the Mongaup River in New York.

The following strange tales are more unexplained mysteries- mainly about "Little People." These tales of the Little People come from the Catskill Mountains in Upstate New York and have been gathered from people who live in the region.

Over the years, dozens of people have sent me their personal encounters or tales of little people they once heard from family members. These stories may sound unbelievable, but they were quite real to those who experienced these events.

The Mysterious Mirror

During my numerous years of traveling and exploring I've heard countless strange tales. This one is by far the weirdest.

On August 1917, Grandma May passed away. She had arrived from England several years earlier, and was living with her grandson George and family. After being laid to rest, George remembered the old mirror she brought with her across the sea. It still was in the attic gathering dust. The frame was quite unique. It was almost four inches wide and made with great craftsmanship.

Weeks later it was removed and placed against a tree in the back yard. After being cleaned, George entered the house for dry towels. Upon his return he discovered it had moved and was now against the fence. Both children denied touching the mirror.

It was hung above the fireplace where it remained. One day, his wife Jill saw it hanging crooked and straightened the out old mirror. Later that month, it was discovered on the floor beside a chair. Once more it was returned to its rightful place. Jill jokingly said, "Perhaps it's haunted by Grandma's ghost." How wrong she was.

Months later the mirror was moved to the hall. One day while he looked at it, George noticed a transparent picture that slowly covered his reflection. As he gazed, the picture of a tranquil country scene covered the mirror's face. The landscape was rolling grassy hills covered with trees. Nearby, there was a small gurgling stream that ran beside some rocks.

From one side, two small people appeared about three feet tall. They sat besides the stream and were talking. Each wore odd-looking clothes and appeared to be a boy and girl of teenage years. Moments later, the boy happened to look in George's direction. He acted quite startled. He pointed toward him and both ran off.

At that second the scene vanished and the mirror returned to normal. George related his strange experience to Jill. She thought it was a combination of light, shadows and a good dose of wild imagination.

Throughout the months, George would occasionally pause beside the mirror, but nothing odd appeared. When both parents passed away, Bill their son, heard the tale numerous times while growing up. He moved the mirror to his home. Bill's sister wanted nothing to do with the spooky thing, as she called it.

It hung on his wall over the years and nothing out of the ordinary occurred. The tale told by his Dad was mentioned several times among close friends and relatives.

One spring day, Bill approached the old mirror and stood quite close. Without realizing why, he gazed intently into it. Suddenly, the same scene described by his father appeared. Two small children sat beside the stream. Once again, the boy looked toward Bill's direction and both ran off.

Only this time the scene didn't fade. Bill continued to look at the peaceful surroundings. The boy reappeared and walked cautiously toward his side of the mirror. He came quite close and gazed up at Bill. The boy smiled, backed off, waved and ran away.

What logical explanation could be given to explain this fantastic chain of events over the years. When the mirror mysteriously moved was it trying to draw attention to itself so somebody would gaze intently into its domain? For what purpose?

Where did Grandma May find this strange oddity? Why didn't she ever tell George about its strange powers? Why was it stored alone in the dusty attic away from view? Why did both witness the same scene years apart? So many questions, so little answers.

This mysterious mirror now hangs on the wall of a relative's home somewhere in New York. Nothing unusual has happened since Bill's encounter many years ago. Occasionally, a family member gazes "briefly" into the haunting mirror. But, nothing is seen except ones own reflection. Is the mirror waiting patiently for someone to gaze longer into its world?

If all this is true, where did the odd mirror originate and how old must it be? Where is this land of peaceful scenery? Does it exist only in the viewers mind? Or is the mirror a doorway into another time or dimension? If we knew the answers to everything, life would become rather dull. Don't you agree?

The Phantom Car

Scattered across southern California are many lonely deserts such as the Borrego Badlands, west of the Salton Sea. The great Mojave and others like the area near the Chocolate Mountains, now a Gunnery Range, are closed to the general public.

Like others regions throughout the Southwest, all have their legends of lost mines and mysterious happenings. One particular tale involves an old Model T Ford.

Jack and two friends, Hank and Don were four wheeling and exploring the desert sands southeast of Indio. The time was during the mid 1970's, I'm told. Jack always carried his metal detector, as there was always a chance to find something – old mining tools, perhaps a rusted gun or other items hidden among the sands.

By late afternoon they came upon a group of rock outcroppings, at times, used by fleeing outlaws to hide their ill-gotten loot. They would return months later when things had cooled down.

They stopped and searched the surrounding area. But, nothing of value was found. However, a box of old dynamite was discovered between two rocks. It looked as though it had been there for many years and was unstable, as beads of nitro covered each stick. There were around ten in the wooden box. If dropped, it could go off.

It was decided to blow the dangerous power-up before someone else stumbled across the deadly cargo.

Jack, himself a weekend prospector, had some fuse and blasting caps in his truck. After he lit the one-minute fuse, all ran for cover. At that moment an old Model T Ford appeared from out of nowhere and headed in their direction. Hank ran and waved his arms to signal the driver to stop. Too late, the charge went off and knocked Hank to the ground.

After the smoke and dust cleared they expected to find wreckage of the truck, and perhaps a body. But, nothing was there. They couldn't believe what just occurred before their eyes.

While back in Indio, they mentioned the strange incident to several locals. One old timer told them an interesting tale. Years before, a miner known as

Tom, had lived in the hills. He worked a small gold claim, and dug out enough to keep the wolf from his door. One day he was found dead behind the wheel of his Ford. It appeared he died from a heart attack while driving.

Some claim his ghost can still be seen driving his Model T Ford across the hills, day or night. It was coming from nowhere and heading to nowhere. Perhaps, Tom doesn't realize he's dead and still travels the lonely deserts. Did Jack and the others witness Tom making his trip across the flats that late afternoon?

There are tales of ghost ships sailing the seas, and phantom trains traveling on old rusted tracks no longer in use. They why not old Model T Fords?

Lady On A Train

During October 2006, an interesting letter arrived from a woman who had a strange experience while on a train in 1948. Her encounter with the little ones occurred while on her way to visit her mother.

After reading awhile, Sue set the book aside. She sat and gazed out of the window at the passing scenery as the old train rattled along the tracks. A dirt road ran parallel with the tracks for several miles before it turned northward.

Still looking out across the open country, she spotted five extremely small people beside the road. All were looking in her direction with the speed of the train. It lasted but several seconds.

Less then a minute later, the same five appeared again at a different location further down the tracks. Sue almost pulled her neck out to get a better view. The tallest was perhaps two feet in height, while the others were much smaller.

An elderly lady who sat behind her leaned forward

and asked, "You saw them, didn't you?"

She then moved to the empty seat beside Sue. "I ride this train quite often and see them occasionally. Even the conductor and others have spotted the little group." Sue, surprised by what she was saying, asked, "Who are they?" The old woman smiled and continued, "They were a family of five with two daughters and a son. They lived back in the woods where you saw them."

"When these tracks were being laid, the workers camped at the rail site. One afternoon two of them became real drunk. There was a rumor of a family of little people lived just south of the camp a short way back into the forest. These two, quite intoxicated came upon their dwelling while they stumbled about the trees.

Both believed these creatures were evil spirits or little devils. One spotted movement near a window and called out, "Come out you freaks." When no reply was heard, they set fire to the small house. It went up like dry tender. Screams came from within. Several tried to escape but were caught and thrown back into the blazing flames while they laughed.

When this dreadful crime was uncovered the two responsible were caught and held for the local sheriff. What became of them afterward wasn't mentioned.

Several of the crew went to the scene and discovered five little bodies among the ruins. A single grave was dug and all were laid to rest. No marker was placed at the gravesite.

Many years later, a gentleman from some university arrived at the location. Finding the burnt remains, he placed a wooden cross nearby. Try as he may, the burial site wasn't found. It was suspected, by many, that he was there on the sole purpose to find the site.

On Sue's return a week later, she witnessed nothing unusual along the route.

Here we have a rather interesting, but sad, tale of little people who perished in flames set by two crazy drunks.

One question, why would the spirits of this family appear at different sites? In this letter the name of the state where this occurred wasn't mentioned.

Is this odd tale true or just an urban legend? Was
this a family of extremely small people who
decided to live away from us, giants, they knew
could only bring them harm, and did?

Has this area today been turned in urban sprawl
and covered with homes, schools, apartments and
shopping centers? I hope the grave, if it does exist,
wasn't disturbed during construction.

Perhaps it's located in someone's back yard
beneath the green cool grass where children play.

Clint Walker's UFO

My friend, Clint Walker, the star of the old TV series, "Cheyenne," told me an interesting story about his first UFO sighting back in 1951.

At the time, he was traveling the Mississippi River Road back in Illinois. The river also paralleled the roadway and had some high cliffs nearby. It was empty of traffic, but occasionally a car would pass.

An odd sight greeted Clint as he glanced off toward the river. Coming toward him, above the water, was a saucer shaped UFO. It was perhaps twenty-five feet across and dull silver in color.

Slowing down, Clint saw it pause for several seconds about a hundred and twenty feet from him. It then moved slowly toward the cliffs where it rose up until it reach the summit. It then moved away and out of sight.

Clint, and wife Susan now live in Central California. He's one of the nicest persons you'd ever want to meet.

The Navajo UFO

Another short but intriguing story supposedly occurred on the Navajo Indian Reservation in Northern Arizona toward the end of 2004.

Two young men, both in their mid-twenties, were on their way home to Polacca, Washington. In the distance they spotted a reflection and rode off to investigate.

Approaching the area they came upon a large UFO resting on the desert sands some hundred yards away. It had no windows only a red light atop a small dome. The craft was some fifty feet across and silver in color.

Leaving their horses, both approached the strange craft. As they did, both heard a sound like something closing. At that moment the UFO rose up, then moved off toward the west traveling about a hundred feet off the ground. It then sped off and disappeared in several seconds.

The only visible proof the object that was there,

was a large circular depression left in the soft sand. Just south of the circle several scuffmarks were discovered which could have been made from footwear.

THIS IS WHAT THE APPARITION COULD HAVE
RESEMBLED FROM THE DESCRIPITION GIVEN

Apparition of Carmen

The Apparition of Carmen [4]

This mysterious tale was related to us back in '57. During this period, we had spent a considerable amount of time in the mountains several miles west of Carmen, a small roadside community located between Tubac and Tumacacori, Arizona.

Our partner Roy knew several people in the immediate vicinity. While he visited one of his friends, after he purchased supplies at Tubac, he told us the following story.

A Mexican family residing in Carmen, whose name I have long since forgotten, had put their six-year-old daughter to bed around seven one night. Her parents then settled down for the evening. They listened to the radio and finished some last-minute chores.

It was exceptionally quiet that night and not even

---

4 Note: This story is republished from Southern Arizona Trails, Vol. 3, No. 82, May 3, 1988, Page 22.

their neighbor's dog would bark as it usually would. Also, there was a heavy stillness in the air. Several hours later, their daughter let out a scream, and broke the silence.

Both hurried into her room and expected to find she had fallen from the bed or had a disturbing dream. Little Maria, as we'll call her, was kneeling in the center of the bed, crying and trembling. She pointed toward the single window in the room.

After she was quieted down some, her mother asked what was wrong.

Maria said she had awakened and saw a yellow glow coming through the window. Then, she spotted a ghostly apparition that looked directly at her. Different colored small balls of flickering lights drifted lazily around its head. When she cried out, it slowly faded from view.

Both parents agreed she must have been dreaming. Afterward, her father took a light and searched around the house to assure little Maria that nothing was out there. He found nothing unusual as the beam cut through the surrounding darkness, and revealed only the scattered mesquite trees and nearby cactus. He did, however, feel uneasiness in the night air.

He returned inside. Maria still insisted she had seen the strange flowing yellow specter. It was past 10 o'clock before the frightened girl again drifted off to sleep.

The parents retired to their bedroom and were asleep by 11. A short while later, the mother awoke with a feeling of impending danger. She thought this was brought about by Maria's frightening experience earlier.

She glanced toward her daughter's partly opened door and froze in fear. From within the room, she saw a light yellow glow. With trembling hands, she shook her husband until he awoke.

They crept silently toward the door and gazed in disbelief. Floating gently outside the window peering in was the apparition described by little Maria. The mother grabbed the small crucifix hanging around her neck and crossed herself while still transfixed by the mysterious sight before her.

The ghostly specter was looking down at the sleeping girl with both its arms outstretched at its sides.

Tiny balls of colored lights were seen dancing slowly around its upper body. From what they could see of its features, it was difficult to determine if the glowing phantom was male or female.

It must have sensed their presence, as its large white eyes, with small black pupils slowly looked up at them. Gathering all his courage, the father ran for the door and darted around the house. As he came around the corner, the apparition slowly drifted over the land toward the west. As it reached a high point, the glowing figure vanished. The strange hovering night visitor was never seen again.

A great amount of speculation can be injected into this odd encounter.

Was it truly a ghost? If so, what about the dancing lights? In the numerous stories I've read about such sightings, never did I hear about balls of hovering colored lights accompanying the spirits. Could there also be some religious overtones here?

Finally, there is always the possibility the strange thing could have been some type of "E.T." It might have landed over the nearby ridge and decided to see what us earth folks really look like really close. Perhaps that was the reason it returned twice. The lights could have been some kind of energy field that surrounded it, but this is only speculation offered by several individuals I know.

If little Maria had seen the figure, I'd say it was her imagination or a bad dream. I'd be somewhat skeptical but I would listen to the story with an open mind. When all three spotted the thing, then it's time for some deep serious thinking.

During the last few years I've come to believe that almost anything is possible. That famous quote comes to mind: "There are more things in heaven and earth than are dreamt of in your philosophy."

Jimmy Talltree

Jimmy Talltree

This story is rather short but quite unique. An Indian, Jimmy Talltree, once told this tale to Ben Johnson, a noted western actor who has appeared in many feature films. Ben retired to Phoenix, Arizona and past away several years ago.

This remarkable story occurred sometime during 1950 or '51 in the extreme northern section of New York. Jimmy, supposedly of Mohawk blood, worked by cutting and selling wood to the locals.

While he fished beside a nearby river, he caught several. At noon, he fried two of them and left the other in the pan beside the fire. The aroma drifted over the area and ignited the taste buds of anything nearby. Jimmy returned to his old truck to obtain more bread.

On his return, he spotted a little man making off with the last fish. He gave chase but lost the little thief among the thicket.

Since childhood, Jimmy has heard tales from the elders about the little people living in the remote forests.

This friendly Indian was honest and truthful. If Jimmy said he saw a little man, then, he saw a little man. There was no question about it.

Jimmy had an idea. Weeks later, he again returned to his fishing spot.

After catching two fish. He left one on the grass then returned to the truck and waited awhile.

On his return, sure enough, the fish was missing. Did the little criminal steal it? Then again, an animal hidden nearby could have taken it while Jimmy was gone.

Nobody has seen Jimmy since late 1997. Perhaps he has passed away. Or, is he still fishing and sharing his catch with the little fellow? There are so many fantastic stories and so little hard evidence.

The Runner and the Dust Devil

The Runner and the Dust Devil

Utah, 1977. Ben and his close friend, Steve, were out exploring the sandstone country of this picturesque state. After they hiked, took photos and enjoyed the peaceful surroundings, they made camp among some boulders. As the sun bedded down for the night, the sandstone formations took on a deep orange color.

The following morning, both hiked northward across the sand. About noon, a strong wind began to kick up and gusts approached well over twenty miles an hour. The winds would subside then hit again with a vengeance.

Steve spotted a small cave among the sandstone cliffs. They stumbled toward the opening and hoped to find shelter from the blowing wind.

While they sat near the cave entrance, they both caught sight of somebody running across the open terrain. As the individual grew closer something looked odd. Looking through their binoculars, this is what they observed, according to them.

The man wore soft appearing boots. A bright red lion cloth covered both front and back. His headpiece consisted of round beads of various colors.

Around both arms were many circular rings. He had long hair, was quite tall, and well built.

This description was taken while looking through field glasses, as the strange man was some two hundred yards away.

As the runner moved along something resembling a small dust devil was seen moving with him as if it had intelligence. If the man slowed, so did the dust devil. If he changed direction, so did the whirling dust cloud. It resembled a race between two cross-country runners.

At one time, the man paused and looked around, as if he didn't know where he was. The dust devil circled him until he once again moved on. It was the craziest thing both had ever witnessed.

The two friends noticed the strong wind had

diminished when the stranger first appeared. By now the "two" had covered some four hundred yards as they moved north. Reaching a high rise both disappeared over its edge and disappeared.

Ben had the presence of mind to take three pictures of the odd event before it ended. Another friend of Ben's said he saw the pictures once. Ben used his telephoto lens to capture the scene. The image covered about sixty percent of the picture. That would show great deal of the man and his dusty partner.

Where did he originate? Surely, not our world. Did he somehow arrive with the wind? Was the swirling dust devil a form of intelligence? It did move beside him as both raced across the sand.

Was our mystery runner from another dimension, and arrived here by accident? If so, I hope he and his windy companion eventually found their way home.

Out of hundreds of stories I've heard since 1956, this story, plus several others are the most intriguing.

He Left No Tracks

This rather unique story arrived last December from a lady living in New Mexico. She wanted to share this short tale with others.

It's entirely true and occurred during a visit with her son Allan and his wife Connie, in Connecticut one winter.

While both were at work, Grace finished several chores needed around the house. She was from New Mexico and disliked the bitter cold of the northeast. But, it was the only time she could visit.

Outside snow covered the ground and trees and a grey unfriendly sky hung over the landscape. By noon a light snow began falling. About thirty feet at the rear of the house, which stood on acreage as they lived in a rural community, was a hill some ten feet high. Several years earlier, Allan built a gazebo at the top.

Grace was standing at a window looking toward the hill. At first she thought a small animal had taken shelter within the structure.

She found a pair of binoculars on the desk and looked toward the hill. She then gasped in amazement. The object was a little man just over a foot in height. He appeared cold and looked around somewhat bewildered. He stepped from the gazebo and sank into the snow up to his waist.

Grace couldn't take her eyes off this strange scene that unfolded before her. She knew the others would never believe her, so she searched frantically for her camera. After she found it, Grace rushed back to the window, but the little fellow had disappeared.

Upon there return, she related the strange tale to Allan and Connie. Both smiled with her son, saying. It was an animal of some kind. "No," replied his mother, "What I saw through the glasses was a little man and nothing else. He looked disorientated. Like he didn't realize where he was." Later, they checked the hill. Sure enough, a hole was seen. But no tracks were discovered coming or going from it.

Another little man lost in the winter snow. Quite similar to my other story, "A Cold November

Day." How he arrived atop the hill without leaving tracks is another unsolved mystery.

In theory, this might have occurred: he fell through a slip in time and space from another world or dimension by accident. One moment he was standing in his world, then BINGO. He drops into ours on the snow-covered hill. The poor guy can't realize how he arrived there. Seconds later, BINGO, he's back to his world, telling a fantastic yarn, nobody believes. They might have thought differently if he had arrived covered in snow.

If all the stories we hear about little people and other strange creatures are indeed true, we surely live in one wild, wonderful, crazy world where almost anything can occur and usually does.

Ghosts, lake monsters, UFO's, aliens, Bigfoot, giants, little people, things that go bump in the night, other dimensions, worlds, time travel, the hollow earth and government cover ups – the list is almost endless.

Almost every year a new mystery creeps out from under the woodwork. Will it ever end? I hope not. It's too much fun waiting for something new to appear or seeing an ugly peering in through a window during a dark, windy night, or spotting a winged something or other flying through the skies.

We indeed live in a strange world with stranger things existing around us. Magic lands, magic wizards, magic crystals, magic music, magic creatures, magic words, magic dragons and magic wells.

Is all of this true or only a figment of our imagination? Let's hope we're wrong.

The Rock Garden

The Rock Garden

Time and place: July 1975, somewhere south of the Adirondack Mountain Range located in upstate New York.

Mike and Janice, a young couple, just returned from a wonderful vacation to Long Island, New York after they visited close friends and family members.

Several days later while working near their rock garden, Janice noticed things didn't look quite the same. Some stones were moved and a few flowers had been transplanted to other locations.

She called to Mike and he also saw the change. They thought neighborhood children were responsible. But, none resided in the area. Soon the incident was forgotten as nothing had been damaged.

A few weeks later, the garden once again had been altered. Flowers were moved elsewhere and small stones now encircled a flowerpot. Both decided somebody was playing a joke on them, but who?

It surely wasn't their close neighbors, as they have known them for years.

After a light rain shower, Janice came upon small tracks in the wet earth near the rock garden. They didn't resemble raccoon tracks but looked more human in appearance. They were perhaps two inches in length, and each had five toes. Later, Mike took several pictures of the odd tracks.

Three nights later, both caught sight of a soft white light radiating from the direction of the garden some twenty feet from the picture window. The light was circular and perhaps a foot in diameter.

Moving within the glow was a little girl about a foot tall. She wore a long white dress and dark hair hung well below her shoulders. She seemed to be rearranging the nearby foliage.

Both gazed in disbelief at the strange scene that unfolded before them. The little night visitor worked rapidly. Then, suddenly, she and the light vanished. Janice called her friend, Jill, who lived nearby. She told Jill about her mysterious encounter.

The following evening, Jill arrived just before

dark. She was smart enough to bring a camera. Nothing occurred that night. But, two nights later, the girl made her second appearance shortly after 10 PM.

She called her friend once again. Jill entered from the rear door. She also witnessed the mysterious scene that played out beside the garden. Not being a professional photographer, she made an inexcusable error. She didn't realize that a pane of glass separated her from the ongoing activity outside as she snapped off one picture. The only thing she caught on the film was the reflection of the flash that bounced back from the windowpane. Seconds later, both girl and light vanished.

From that time on our little night intruder never returned. Maybe, she was frightened off by the camera's sudden flash.

Who was this strange night visitor, and why the interest in the rock garden? This harmless creature arrived for a brief period of time. He then left like a gentle summer breeze across the peaceful countryside never to return, as far as we know. We know so little of the unknown that occupies this small, insignificant little lonely planet we have come to call Earth.

The River Boy

The River Boy

Billy, age thirteen, loved to hike and find hidden places within the surrounding forests, especially, during summer months.

His favorite retreat was beside the Mongaup River, which begins its journey from Swan Lake further north.

This slow moving river has depths from six inches to a foot or more. Its picturesque route cuts through unpopulated areas. Billy would paddle his bike along the road and parked it among the trees. From this point he hikes to the river below. During warm days he enjoyed lying in a shallow section of the river.

He felt the cool water gently flow over his body. It was a relaxing location and he came there several times a week. The only sounds were the peaceful movement of the water or a birdcall. For a lad of his age this was quite unusual, as he loved tranquility.

Glancing toward the riverbank, Billy caught sight

of something moving among the brush. He lay motionless hoping to see some woodland animal. Stepping from behind the foliage came a little girl. Now that's a first. Usually, it's a little man with beard and a sloppy hat.

She was quite tiny – well under a foot in height. If she was of normal size she could pass for any young girl of sixteen or so.

Billy blinked his eyes several times but she was still there. Her clothing was rather old and worn, but well kept and clean. From his low level he couldn't observe if the tiny creature had shoes.

Unknowingly, Billy half submerged our little Miss as he knelt and drank from the river. Billy was transfixed at the scene that unfolded before him. Next, she turned her head quickly, as if she heard something nearby and then stood.

As she looked toward the river, their eyes met. Perhaps the little one thought Billy was some "River Goddess" living in the water. Both couldn't take their eyes off one another. The girl then walked slowly backwards. After she reached the safety of the trees, she disappeared.

Billy stood and approached the location where she had been, but nothing was heard nor seen. Billy gathered his cloths and returned home shaken some, but not scared.

He told his parents, but they didn't believe his tale, like most don't. She said he must have fallen asleep and dreamed the entire thing. Billy replied, "No way, Mom. If I was asleep I might have drowned or woke up gasping for breath. What I saw was real."

Throughout the summer, Billy occasionally returned to the location of the encounter. But, he never saw the tiny girl again. Billy, now thirty, stil insists it actually occurred.

I wonder who she was and where she came from, out there alone among the unfriendly forests. If the tale is indeed true, it must have been a wonderful experience for Billy. He still lives in the vicinity and visits that tranquil site occasionally. But, he doesn't lie in the cool running water during summer months, as he once did so long ago.

The Surprise

Ted was employed as a Sewer Worker, better known in the trade as a Sanitation Engineer. He and friend, Ray, had been partners for several years. During this time both had seen almost everything in the sewers.

December of 1997 found them below Twenty Second Street working on a minor problem. Afterward they headed for the opening above to have lunch. From behind them they heard a voice cry out. They headed in that direction to answer the distress call and came upon a strange site.

There, caught in the water, was a little man. No bigger than two feet tall. Ted reached down and pulled him to safety. He resembled a drowned rat. His long hair hung dripping with water, and he kept coughing and seemed confused where he was.

Ray turned toward, Ted and asked, "Have we been drinking today? If not, what is that?" Ted's reply was, "I see it, but I don't believe it."

Ted knelt down and asked who he was. But there

was no answer. He had gray clothing and moccasin-like footwear. At first he didn't appear to be afraid of his rescuers. But that would change quite soon.

Suddenly, the little runt came back to reality. Looking up, he saw Ted and Ray standing over him like two menacing giants.

He let out a scream and fled down the tunnel. Ted glanced towards Ray and asked, "Are we going to tell anybody about this?"

"Hell no," answered Ray, "I want to keep my job. How about you?"

"I didn't see a thing," replied Ted.

First, is the story true? Both claim it is. Upon telling their wives later, both accused them of being drunk or pulling a hoax. They also agreed not to mention it to anybody.

Their children, of course, never heard the tale. If so, the story would have been all over the school grounds.

There is a theory these little ones exist in another dimension and pop into our world occasionally.

Perhaps, they mistakenly drop into odd places, like onto a car roof, as in Chapter 22, of my book, *"Little People,"* or, into a dark wet sewer. No wonder the little guy, was screaming. I hope he made it back home.

Pam's Friend

Time and location: 1935, central New York. Pam, age six, was playing beside the house with several dolls. Her mother, Jan was cleaning up after lunch. Russ, her husband, had just completed a few minor chores. Unbeknownst to this family their tranquil day would end like no other.

As Russ stepped outside to check the mail, Pam came by and headed for her room to collect more dolls. Russ returned to the house and noticed a raggedly doll standing beside the others some twenty odd feet away. He wondered why his daughter would keep such an unkempt plaything.

Then, all of a sudden this gray clothed doll turned, and looked directly at him. It wasn't a doll at all, but a small, rather plump little man.

He stood perhaps a foot in height. Russ almost dropped the mail as the little guy ran off toward the barn. At that same moment, Pam stepped outside. When she saw what was happened, she yelled, "Daddy, you scared "T-T" away. He's my friend."

Jan, who heard the excitement, came to the door, but it was to late for her to see the little fellow. He had already vanished into the shadows of the woods.

After she heard the wild story that Russ had described, she turned to Pam and asked, "Do you play with that creature?"

"Yes," replied Pam, "He lives way back in the forest. His name is T-T."

Jan still couldn't quite fathom the idea of such little things that exist within the surrounding countryside. But, she believed what her husband had witnessed. Jan forbid Pam to play or go near the little man ever again, as he might have germs.

As days turned into weeks the small gentleman occasionally would be seen under the trees or near there barn. But, he kept his distance from the house. After awhile he became a permanent fixture around the property. They began feeling sorry for the lonely guy and began leaving food outside.

Russ remembered their old neighbor, Jim, telling them one time about little people living in the hills. Russ smiled and said, "Guess, old Jim was right. I saw one, and our daughter had one for a playmate."

Pam never played with the little rascal again, but was seen waving at him several times. As fall approached, their little friend left, never to be seen again.

This fantastic story was never mentioned to family members or friends. It was their secret. Besides, none would have believed them.

As Pam grew older, she told her parents T-T spoke funny and she couldn't understand him but they managed to get along. He just wanted to be friends with her.

The tale, above, was told by an elderly lady who lived in a nursing home. Some believe it was Pam herself.

Is this story true, or a figment of the old lady's imagination?

The Wild Bunch

The Wild Bunch

It seems Canada is getting into the act of seeing little people on their side of the border. Apparently these wee folks don't recognize international boundaries. Or, they could be Canada's homegrown version of these elusive people.

The time of this encounter is May of 2004. The story is from, Kirk W., a Canadian from Montreal. Kirk and wife, Diane, were returning from visiting her ailing father. Up ahead they spotted two women who jumped from a parked car and waved frantically as both ran toward them. In belief that an accident had occurred, Kirk stopped beside the road.

As these wild-eyed women approached, Diane opened the door. Both talked uncontrollably and it made it impossible to understand what had happened. After they calmed both, the older lady told this amazing tale.

After driving home from a day of shopping, both saw six or seven little men scrambling across the road jumping and dancing. Hitting the brakes,

Helen, the driver yelled out, "Did you see that?"

"Yes," came her passenger's reply. The little guys vanished back into the surrounding woods.

Moments later, another small group emerged from the trees then ran back among the shadows. For their size, these tiny men moved quite rapidly. Three came charging out, stopped, looked at the car briefly and then returned to the forest.

These were the traditional little men so often seen further south in New York. They were a foot or so tall, beards, sloppy hats and shaggy looking clothing.

One brave little maverick actually jumped on the hood of her car with ease. He came close to the front window, looked around, smiled, and then leaped to the ground and disappeared into the brush. They rolled up the windows in expectation of a full frontal attack from these wild devils. But, none came. All this madness lasted perhaps two minutes. At this point, Kirk's truck came into view.

After he heard this amazing story, Kirk walked to the location of the mayhem. While no little men were seen, he did see lots of movement among the surrounding brush.

Apparently, the gang was having a party. But, why so near a busy road? Could they have found a half full bottle of wine or whiskey near the road, sampled its contents, and it set them off to their wild ways, rarely witnessed by humans?

Diane suggested they might have seen squirrels or other small animals running about. "No way," said, Lori, the passenger, "I've been married three times and I know men when I see them. These were little wild men."

We are surrounded by many mysteries that we'll never solve. It would be a sad world if everything were already known. Life wouldn't be fun anymore. True or not, this wild yarn is quite amazing.

The Mountain Cabin

The Mountain Cabin

Rick and Joyce have a weekend mountain cabin some twenty miles from their home. This hideaway is nestled among the trees and the nearest neighbor was perhaps a mile west.

The young couple had inherited the cabin from Joyce's grandmother years earlier. During a three-day holiday they loaded the car and headed toward their retreat. They arrived at the property around noon. While, Rick carried in the suitcases, his wife prepared lunch.

Early the following morning, Joyce was tending to their flower garden, while Rick was removing several low tree limbs that were rubbing against a windowpane.

Around mild-noon both sat and relaxed on the front porch with some coffee. Suddenly, a small stone landed at their feet. Joyce looked up and expected to see a squirrel among the branches that was the culprit. But, none were seen.

Moments later, a second stone bounced off the

handrail. Once again nothing was seen above. Joyce jokingly said, "Perhaps the little varmint doesn't want us this close to its nest."

"The little stinker is declaring war on us," replied Rick with a smile. At that instant another stone hit the porch deck and bounced down the steps. Looking up with searching eyes, Joyce was calling out, "Now, you stop that."

Both stood gazing upward when a little face appeared and peered down at them from among the leaves. Joyce cried out, "Oh my God, it's a human face." Indeed. It was a little man with a sloppy hat, beard, large eyes and displaying a wide smile.

They couldn't believe their own eyes. Rick, quite excited, said, "Damn, it's one of those little people we've heard so much of." The tiny face pulled back behind the leaves until he was out of sight. Both watched as the small shadowy figure climbed through the branches then jumped onto the cabin roof down the other side and disappeared into the surrounding brush.

The question is – why did he drop the stones? He didn't mean to injure them, as none of the stones hit the couple. Was he playing with them and wanted to be spotted?

Most of them refrain from human contact, and usually flee when seen. This friendly fellow broke the mold for reasons we might never know. Perhaps he wanted us to know they are still around. Sightings of these mysterious beings have diminished for several years.

Our couple reports no new sightings of their smiling friend. But, believe it, he's still around watching them. If he wants to become friends, perhaps he'll come someday a knocking at their front door. This interesting tale occurred July 2007.

On the Trail

On the Trail

George, a levelheaded lad of nineteen, was out hiking in the vicinity of those mysterious mountains known as the Catskills in Upstate New York where many strange happenings occur throughout the years.

On Friday, he had an argument over something trivial with his girlfriend, Pat. Our young man knew the quarrel was his fault as he hiked the picturesque trail through the quiet forest.

He arrived at a junction in the trail and decided to take the left branch. In doing so, it would lead him into an encounter with the unknown.

Near noon, George stopped for lunch and sat beneath some trees just off the patch. From his vantage point he could gaze out across the peaceful rolling green hills. As he reached for his canteen, George heard several voices from down the trail. Just then, four little men of small stature, about eighteen inches in height, appeared.

They each wore gray, ragged clothing and soft hats. Three had beards, but the fourth was clean-shaven. The little foursome hadn't noticed George at first as he sat among the surrounding foliage. They spoke in some foreign language that George couldn't recognize.

The small group of strangers must have sensed his presence as they looked in his direction and stopped. At that moment, it felt as though time itself froze. He couldn't hear nor could he move. It was the most unusual sensation he ever experienced.

When this odd feeling left, the little guys were nowhere to be seen. George picked up his pack and looked both ways along the trail. No sign of them anywhere.

Upon hearing his remarkable tale, his family and friends believed he fell asleep and dreamed the entire incident. Poor George couldn't convince them otherwise. But, one among them would soon be a believer.

Once more back with Pat, they returned to the site of the encounter with the little ones several weeks later. While at the location, both heard little voices from among the trees. As they grew closer, they didn't stay to investigate, but hurriedly left the area, quite shaken.

As I read one time, "What we know could fill several large libraries. What we don't know could fill a dozen or more."

We are surrounded by mysteries everyday. Most will never be solved.

Face at the Window

Face at the Window

L ittle Sue, a pretty girl of five, was playing in her bedroom accompanied by the families rag tail dog, Toy.

Late that afternoon while playing, Toy kept barking towards the window. Sue looked in that direction and was surprised at what her eyes revealed. It was the face of a little man. His legs apparently stood on several branches from a small tree that grew beside the house.

Sue ran to her mother and excitedly told her that she saw a small man who peered in at her from outside. Mother smiled and said it was a squirrel or some other animal. She then continued with her chores.

Being quite persistent about seeing the little fellow, she accompanied her daughter back to the room. Of course, no little stranger was seen.

When things settled down, Sue returned to play. She kept glancing towards the window. She didn't have to wait long. Seconds later, the mysterious figure reappeared. Both looked at each other and smiled.

He resembled most of the other sightings reported in the area– a foot or so tall, sloppy hat and beard.

Our tiny visitor climbed up until he stood on the narrow ledge and looked in. Sue slid from her bed and walked slowly toward the window.

Toy sat besides her and watched the little guy with a puzzled expression on his furry-looking face.

The little one looked curiously about the room at the dog, the colorful surroundings, and especially at the girl with the wide smile.

Sue called out, "Mamma, mamma, come quick. The little man is back."

The only response from the other room was, "It's all your imagination. Stop disturbing me."

Once more our little guest retreated back down the tree and vanished from view. Just then, her father drove up and parked beside the house.

As he entered the kitchen, he called out for Sharon, his wife. There was a sound of urgency to his voice as she entered, "What's wrong, Tim?"

Her husband told the following:

As he stepped from his car, he saw a little man, perhaps a foot in height, who ran across the lawn toward the wooded area. The little rascal glanced back at him before he disappeared among the shadows. Sue said, "Mamma, I told you I saw a little man at my window."

Upon hearing her incredible tale, both parents looked at each other in amazement, and then, at the smiling daughter.

Sue, now twenty-eight, still recalls that magical afternoon when she stepped into that unknown world of the little people.

The Little Runners

The Little Runners

June, a young girl of twelve, lived in a small rural area. Each day she walked to school, about half a mile away with several friends. One morning she was running late so they left without her.

Minutes later, June picked up her lunch box, kissed her mother then hurried down the dirt road. To the right was a large grassy field. A rickety wooden fence separated her from the rolling meadow.

To her astonishment, June spotted two little people, perhaps eighteen inches high running across the field. It looked as though it was a boy and girl. Both noticed her but acted as though she wasn't there.

June called out, but received no response from the tiny pair. She crossed the fence and ran toward the fleeing couple as she still called. But again, there was no reaction to her friendly gesture.

Just then, both stopped and looked directly at June. Then, they vanished. Moments later, they had reappeared further away and then disappeared into a wooded area.

After telling her teacher what occurred, she accused her of making up the tale as an excuse for being late.

During lunch period, June told her friends the story and insisted it was true. But like most others, they only laughed at her tall tale.

Now at age thirty-seven, June maintains her story is completely true. She did in fact see the tiny couple running across the grassy meadow.

A child's imagination, or was it a factual encounter with these mysterious little beings?

Caught with his pant down.

Caught With His Pants Down

M ark, age twenty-eight, was out exploring the backcountry near Lake Luzerne located in northern New York during early spring of 1967, so this story goes.

He enjoyed the rugged outdoors and spent most of his free time roaming through the wilderness.

While following a small stream, he heard sounds as if somebody was groaning. When he reached an opening in the trees, Mark came upon an unusual sight. He saw a little man just over a foot in height squatting with his back against a rock. His pants were down around his knees. It was quite obvious the gentleman was in the middle of a bowel movement.

When their eyes met, the little guy let out a scream. He pulled up his pants halfway and ran off, leaving a trail behind him.

I look upon this tale with some skepticism. It could very well have occurred. Mark swore this strange encounter is entirely true.

But, few would ever accept it as being real.

After hearing dozens of tales involving these mysterious creatures, I'm almost certain a race of unknown little folks inhabit the haunting hills of this region. Yet, they wish to remain hidden from the outside world.

This humorous story is by far the most amusing one I've ever heard. Poor, little rascal, he got caught with his pants down. What an embarrassing moment that must have been.

A Cold November Day

A Cold November Day

Back in 1989, I received an interesting letter from a lady residing in New York City. Her tale into the world of the little people began during 1939 when she was a young girl.

The majority of these enchanting sightings usually occur during spring and summer season, but rarely during the colder months. Why, some have asked? The snow would be far too deep for them to travel through. But, there are exceptions. This tale falls into that category.

It was late November. It was cold. Ice and snow covered the landscape. Sue, as we'll name her, was outside building a snowman. Her mother later called her that lunch was ready. She entered the kitchen and sat at the table. Soup, sandwich and hot cocoa were on the menu. From her location, Sue could look outside at her unfinished snowman.

After lunch, Sue glanced out the window and was shocked at the site that greeted her. A little man perhaps a foot tall was tried to negotiate his way through the fallen snow that was as deep as he was tall.

Occasionally, his head would pop up as he tried to pull himself from the cold, wet surroundings.

She giggled at his antics as he tried to escape from his difficult situation. Finally, he slowly climbed from the hole and crawled across the surface of the snow and sank in several inches as he moved slowly forward.

Running to her mother, she told her what she had seen. Her response was that must have been a small animal. "No, No," insisted Sue, "It was a little man."

Both returned outside, but there was no sign of any little man. As they checked the area, it was discovered something has tried to make its way through the snow. The tracks ended near a fence. It did appear something climbed the old fence and followed it toward the forest.

One spot in the snow held a small human handprint, but the mother insisted it was that of a baby raccoon.

Our little wanderer somehow got caught out in the winter weather and desperately tried to make his way back home. I hope the rascal did.

Sue, like most others who had the rare privilege to see one of these mysterious wee folks have had difficulty to convince others it actually occurred.

Little Joe

Little Joe

Two prospectors had been working an old gold mine in northern Montana when they experienced a strange encounter with a little man. But, was he the traditional type often seen by some throughout the eastern states?

Jake and Will had been on the mine site for six months. Enough gold was discovered to keep the wolf away from their front door, as some old miners often said.

An old cabin was located near a group of large boulders. It was a hard and difficult way of life, but they enjoyed the challenge. There always was the chance their next blast could uncover that "mother lode" all miners search for. It had occurred at several abandoned mines in the past.

One evening while they relaxed, they heard noises outside. They believed animals were responsible and no more was thought of it. Minutes later, it happened again. Jake picked up a flashlight and swung open the door.

A few yards away stood a little man perhaps two feet tall. He spotted Jake and he darted away into the night.

Jake told Will what he had just seen. His partner burst into laughter, saying, "You saw what, where?" Both searched the area but nothing was seen.

Jake's description of the little figure parallels that of the mysterious little folks seen in New York. But, there were several differences. He had long white hair and a beard, a pointed nose, stood much taller and wore a bright red cap.

Days later while Will was cutting firewood, he also spotted the little guy sitting atop the boulders looking in his direction. When he realized he was observed, he jumped and vanished among the trees.

While in the general store purchasing supplies, Jake mentioned to John, the owner, about seeing the little man. Smiling, John said, "Oh, that's Little Joe, as we call him. Pay him no mind. He's harmless."

John went on. "Joe's been around these parts for

well over forty years. Guess he was curious about you moving onto that old mining claim."

Will grinned, saying, "You gotta be putting us on." "No way," replied John. "My Dad told me about Little Joe when I was just a kid. Some believe the little varmint is ageless. We don't speak of him to outsiders. Don't want any city folks or government people nosing around up here. We all agree to just leave the little fellow alone. At times we put food out for him. You could say he's our mascot."

"You two have been here long enough, so your not outsiders. So, please keep what I've said under your hat, okay?" Both Jake and Will agreed to do so.

John continued, "Come winter, Joe disappears. We believe he hibernates like a bear. Come spring, ole Joe pops up again. You might come across him at the creek, gathering wood or just walking through the forest."

Realizing he's in no danger from the two new miners, Joe still doesn't let them approach him more then twenty feet.

Who he is or where he came from is still unknown.

Is he a different species from them occasionally seen further east?

Many believe these little ones are created within our own minds. If that is the case, then the entire community is having the same hallucination.

But remember, Jake and Will both saw the little guy way before hearing John's tale.

As of 2006, this small town still keeps its secret, and Joe is still seen in the vicinity. Almost all villages tucked away across our nation have their own secrets. Joe's little town is no different.

This remarkable story arrived during 2006. The return address read: John T. Somewhere, Montana. But he did write in the zip code: 59860.

He Talked Funny

He Talked Funny

During Saturday while the mother worked, her older sister, Rose watched her two girls Mindy, age five, and Sandra, age four.

It was a pleasant afternoon. Rose decided to take both to the local park that covered some ten acres. Aunt Rose, as the girls called her, sat and read as the girls played. A wooden fence separated the park from the forest. This wooded area extended several miles northward until it reached a main highway.

Other families and their children were scattered across the green lawn, and near the swings, and so on.

Rose glanced up and noticed both girls were near the fence. It looked as though they were talking to somebody on the opposite side. But, she couldn't see who it was. Rose called and told them to come away from the fence. They smiled and continued to play.

Later, she saw the girls dancing, laughing and rolling around. They seemed to have picked up another playmate. When the other child turned, Rose was shocked. It was a little man with a beard. He wore knee high boots and a blue jacket. There also was something else strange about him. But, she couldn't put her finger on it. Fearing for the children she called them over. At the same time, the little man climbed through the fence and ran back into the trees.

"Who was that person you were playing with?" Mindy smiled and said, "He didn't tell us his name, but he said he lived back in the forest in some secret place."

Sandra looked up and said, "He talked funny." Mindy continued, "He told us he could only stay on our side for a short time."

"On our side" is an interesting statement, Aunt Rose said. They never saw him again. When they played in the park, she told the children to stay away from the fence.

Our world is surrounded with mysteries. Few if any, will ever be solved.

The Mud Ball

The Mud Ball

Back in 1884, Pat O'Leary, age sixteen, had a reputation of telling tall tales and causing mischief around town. If anything out of the ordinary occurred, all eyes would look in Pat's direction.

It never was anything serious, just little annoyances and pranks. He wasn't a bad lad, just a little on the wild side at times. His father ran a livery stable, while his mother ran their small modest home.

One day while he walked home, Pat spotted what appeared to be a little man who stood beside the lonely road. He had heard several tales told by local Indians of little people who lived among the rolling hills.

After they eyeballed each other for a second, the tiny fellow took off into the woods with Pat in hot pursuit. They darted between trees, through bushes, over dead logs and rocks. Pat stumbled several times but the little guy seemed to dance across the terrain with ease.

For his size, perhaps fifteen inches tall, he managed to keep ahead of his pursuer. As they reached the top of a hill, this small man slipped down the grade. As he arrived at a drop off, he fell down about five feet into a river below.

Pat stopped at the edge and began to laugh as the little fellow splashed about. The water was rather shallow, so he stood up, and waved his fist at Pat. With some difficulty, he made his way across the river.

Reaching the opposite bank, he again waved his fist and disappeared among the trees.

Nobody in town believed his incredible story, as Pat was caught too many times telling a falsehood.

Pat returned to the site of the encounter two days later hoping to find evidence that might prove his story. But, nothing was found.

While he sat near the river, he heard sounds to his right. As he turned, a little guy stood only five feet away. Without a word, he threw a lump of thick mud and hitt Pat on his left forehead just above the eye. In a moment, he had vanished back into the safety of the countryside.

Was this mud slinging in retaliation for making him fall into the river?

Once again, the town locals didn't believed his second tale.

Weeks later a small mole appeared on Pat's forehead where the mud ball struck. Was this also part of the little guy's revenge?

Over the years, he swore his stories of the little man were true. Pat passed away at seventy-one, but he still insisted his encounters with the tiny rascal actually occurred.

A Nun's Tale

In upper New York, there are a number of nuns attached to various religious orders. We believe these ladies of the church are highly respected for their honesty and truthfulness. This account into the unknown deals with that belief.

Let's take, Sister Lucy, age mid-sixties, and regarded as a faithful, caring person in the community. One afternoon, while she sat in the convents' flower garden in deep prayer, she heard a sound nearby. She looked in that direction and spotted movement among the growth. She thought perhaps it was a neighbor's dog or cat. Whatever it was remained hidden from view.

Near another stand of foliage, a second shadowy object was observed.

Like a scene out of some fantasy movie, two little men emerged from concealment stopping several feet from her. She couldn't believe what her eyes saw.

Surely they couldn't be the little people often seen

in the surrounding countryside, she thought. But, there, three feet away, stood two such creatures.

Each wore the traditional clothing as described by witnesses. They resembled adult males, perhaps in their forties. The one on her left approached and offered a flower. After placing it before Sister Lucy, he walked slowly backward until he reached his companion.

The second little guy stepped forward and removed a silver cord from around his neck. Attached was a small wooden cross. It measured about an inch and a half in length by an inch wide. A green stone decorated its center. This also was presented to our nun. He nodded politely and then backed away. He reached some hedges and both disappeared among them.

This encounter was related to the Mother Superior who forbidden her to never mention the story to another and to forget it ever occurred.

Why did she insist on keeping the tale a secret? Was she afraid it might interfere with church doctrine? Aren't we all God's children regardless of "size?"

Sister Lucy never saw the cross again after handing it over to her superior.

Why did this strange meeting happen and where is the cross today?

As this tale happened during the mid-forties, it could be almost anywhere within the confines of the convent grounds. Mother Superior passed away about four years after hearing the mysterious story.

This most interesting account came to light when Sister Lucy revealed the story to her younger brother before passing away in 1960.

Once again, what was the purpose of this odd meeting between nun and the little ones? Perhaps they knew she was a person of love and peace and meant their race no harm. Did they know the meaning of the cross and who made it? Answers we'll no doubt never know or understand.

Hearing this remarkable story from a respected Nun gives it veracity.

A Little Man? A Dobby? A Gnome?

A woman from Kingston, New York sent in this photo of an odd scene. She put out a box of clothes and later saw some movement nearby. She snapped the photo above.

This second photo is an enlarged view of his face. [5]

---

[5] Published in *"Fate"* Magazine, July 2007, page 80; September 2007, page 77; and December 2007, page 80. This photo was submitted to *"Fate"* Magazine, by Ron Quinn.

Illustrations

Ron Quinn, author

Ron Quinn has been a prolific writer of treasure hunting and paranormal stories for more than fifty years. He is also the author of *"Little People"* (Galde Press) and *"Searching for Arizona's Buried Treasures"* (BZB Publishing).

Ron, who was born in New York, had his own encounters with little people and discoveries of buried treasures.

After his military release in 1955, he spent two years treasure hunting in Southern Arizona with his brother Chuck and friends, Walter Fisher and Roy Purdie where they uncovered 82 pounds of Spanish gold bars. Ron eventually settled in Tucson, Arizona in 1970 and opened Aztec Film Productions with his brother and produced local TV commercials, travelogues and medical training films.

Ron's great sense of humor is reflected in his stories and especially his cartoons.

Books By Ron Quinn

Besides writing numerous stories, magazine columns and radio interviews, Ron Quinn has published the following books:

"Mysterious Disappearances and Other Strange Tales"
BZB Publishing, Inc (Tucson, Arizona) © 2013

"Searching for Arizona's Buried Treasures"
BZB Publishing, Inc (Tucson, Arizona) © 2013

"Little People"
Galde Press (Lakeville, Minnesota) © 2010

These books are available on Amazon.com and other outlets.

www.ingramcontent.com/pod-product-compliance
Lightning Source LLC
Chambersburg PA
CBHW060848280326
41934CB00007B/967